MW00711373

REVIEWS FOR OTHER GHOST BOOKS BY TROY TAYLOR

In his nearly three dozen volumes, Troy Taylor has consistently managed to mesh his fervent enthusiasm for historical detail with the anecdotal and investigative evidence finding that has won him thousands of loyal readers. Though properly leaning toward the skeptical, Taylor has never once undermined his own sense of wonder at paranormal events and his deep respect for the people who experience them.

URSULA BIELSKI, author of CHICAGO HAUNTS

Troy Taylor's HAUNTED ILLINOIS manages to capture the spookiest aspects of life on the prairie in a way that no other book has done. For those who believe that Illinois is merely corn fields and forests, he only needs to read this book to realize that strange things are lurking on the midwestern plains.

DAVE GOODWIN, author of GHOSTS OF JEFFERSON BARRACKS

Historians and cavers alike will find a wealth of information contained in DOWN IN THE DARKNESS and Taylor, a caver himself, also recounts stories of lost treasure caves and disputed civilizations underground. There is nothing better than a good cave book when you just can't get underground. This book should help you through those desperate times. Put on your helmet, turn down the lights and enjoy a unique journey into the dark, ghost-infested underworld.

PAUL STEWARD - NATIONAL SPEOLOGICAL SOCIETY NEWS

Troy Taylor has brought a new level of professionalism to the field with the GHOST HUNTER'S GUIDEBOOK, which stands as the best and most authoritative book written to date on ghost investigation. Both beginners and experienced investigators alike should make this book their bible... it gives the straight savvy... the material is grounded, practical and informative. It comes as no surprise that Taylor's book has received international praise!

ROSEMARY ELLEN GUILEY, author of ENCYCLOPEDIA OF GHOSTS & SPIRITS

GHOST BOOKS BY TROY TAYLOR

HAUNTED DECATUR (1995)
MORE HAUNTED DECATUR (1996)
GHOSTS OF MILLIKIN (1996 / 2001)
WHERE THE DEAD WALK (1997 / 2002)
DARK HARVEST (1997)
HAUNTED DECATUR REVISITED (2000)
FLICKERING IMAGES (2001)
HAUNTED ILLINOIS (1999 / 2001 / 2004)
SPIRITS OF THE CIVIL WAR (1999)
THE GHOST HUNTER'S GUIDEBOOK (1999 / 2001/ 2004)
SEASON OF THE WITCH (1999/ 2002)
HAUNTED ALTON (2000 / 2003)
HAUNTED NEW ORLEANS (2000)
BEYOND THE GRAVE (2001)
NO REST FOR THE WICKED (2001)
THE HAUNTING OF AMERICA (2001)
HAUNTED ST. LOUIS (2002)
INTO THE SHADOWS (2002)
CONFESSIONS OF A GHOST HUNTER (2002)
HAUNTED CHICAGO (2003)
DOWN IN THE DARKNESS (2003)
FIELD GUIDE TO HAUNTED GRAVEYARDS (2003)
OUT PAST THE CAMPFIRE LIGHT (2004)
THE HAUNTED PRESIDENT (2005)
GHOSTS ON FILM (2005)

WEIRD U.S. (Barnes & Noble Press) (2004)
Co-Author with Mark Moran & Mark Scuerman

WEIRD IL (Barnes & Noble Press) (2005)

COMING SOON

DEAD MEN DO TELL TALES (2006)
by Ursula Bielski & Troy Taylor
GHOSTS BY GASLIGHT (2006)
by Troy Taylor & Ursula Bielski
MYSTERIOUS ILLINOIS
ILLINOIS HAUNTINGS

GHOSTS ON FILM

THE HISTORY, MYSTERY & HOW-TO'S OF SPIRIT PHOTOGRAPHY

BY TROY TAYLOR

GHOSTS ON FILM
History, Mystery & How-to's of
Spirit Photography

Limited Edition Book No. _6_ of 100

- A WHITECHAPEL PRODUCTIONS PRESS PUBLICATION -

For Maggie: They say that unconditional love is like a ghost and that few people will ever see either one... and while you may never see a ghost, you will always know how much your Daddy loves you...

Original Cover Artwork Designed by
© Copyright 2005 by Michael Schwab & Troy Taylor
Visit M & S Graphics at www.manyhorses.com

This Book is Published by:
Whitechapel Productions Press
A Division of Ghosts of the Prairie
P.O. Box 1190 - Decatur, Illinois - 62525
(217) 422-1002 / 1-888-GHOSTLY
Visit us on the Internet at http://www.historyandhauntings.com

First Edition - October 2005
ISBN: 1-892523-41-8

Printed in the United States of America

THE HAUNTED FIELD GUIDE SERIES

Welcome to the new book in a continuing series from Whitechapel Productions Press that will be dedicated to providing the readers with "field guides" to not only haunted places, but to ghost research as well. In the books to come, we will continue to take you beyond the edge of the unknown and provide detailed listings, maps and directions to haunted places all over the Midwest and America, plus additional books on ghost research and more!

We hope that you continue to enjoy the series and that you will journey with us in the future as we take you past the limits of hauntings in America and beyond the furthest reaches of your imagination!

Happy Hauntings!

TABLE OF CONTENTS

INTRODUCTION

One of the greatest potential tools was given to us when photography was invented: for if we could photograph the dead under conditions that carefully exclude trickery, we would surely be so much wiser ---- and the argument for survival would indeed be stronger.
Hans Holzer

The birth of photography and the beginnings of psychical research came within a few decades of one another. Photography, which began as little more than a few tentative experiments in the early 1800's, became commonplace by the middle part of the nineteenth century. It was about this same time when so-called "spirit rappings" began at the Fox family home in Hydesville, New York and launched the Spiritualist movement and the scientific investigations of the movement that followed. By the early 1900's, with the introduction of the Brownie camera, photography had become wildly popular and so had the Spiritualist movement, with séances routinely held in family homes and mediums not only contacting the dead but allegedly taking photographs of the departed as well. It seemed that practically anyone, could "capture" anything at anytime on film. These days, with millions of photographic images being made annually, photography is everywhere and never before has it been as important in the world of ghost research as it is today.

And with all of these photos have come many mysteries, starting in the early days of photography. Some of the questions are historical ones. Who are the people in your old family photographs? Is that man in the photo really Wild Bill Hickok? Is the old photo a copy or one made many years later?

Other questions enter into the world of science. Has the photo been retouched? Does a crime scene photograph distort a distance and create a false impression? Can particular parts of a photo be enhanced?

Finally, for our purposes here, photographs enter into the realm of the supernatural. Could this strange photo be merely a defect of the camera or film? Could that photo of a ghost really be nothing more than a double exposure? What are we really capturing in haunted locations?

This book attempts to provide some of the answers to questions that paranormal researchers have been pondering for some time, representing a wide study of photography as it applies to the ghost research field. As has not been done before, I plan to discuss the historical uses of photography in this field, the uses of photography in actual research and finally how our investigative methods can be applied to the photographs themselves. This guidebook is meant to be a tool that can not only provide an entertaining look at the field of spirit photography and some of the classic photos that have appeared over the years, but also as a tool that can be used in your own investigations. The book will not only look at the most commonly captured types of phenomena that investigators run across but also hints and tips on basic uses for cameras, using cameras in field work and even a guide to ruling out various types of flaws that may look like "ghosts on film" but are not.

Strangely, a lot of what this book will be about is what is not a ghost in your photograph. As skeptics will always maintain --- "extraordinary claims require extraordinary proof" --- and while they usually use this statement to debunk any type of phenomena that they personally don't believe in, there is truth to this maxim as well. One of the goals of this book is to provide you with the tools to examine and analyze your photographs before you put them on display for the world to see and claim that they are evidence of ghosts among us. Let's face it --- there are hundreds, even thousands, of photographs on display on the internet and elsewhere that make the claim of presenting a ghost, or some sort of spirit energy, on film. I will come out and say it in this introduction that the vast majority of them do not!

Hopefully, this book will help you to make intelligent determinations about your own photographs and whether or not they really present anything remarkable --- or if they are merely flaws in your film or some other unremarkable situation. There is a principle that is used in investigative work that maintains that the simplest explanation for something, which is the hypothesis with the fewest assumptions, is most likely to be correct. This does not mean that we should start dismissing any possibly genuine paranormal photos because it would be much simpler not to believe in ghosts but that we start analyzing them by looking for the non-paranormal explanations first. If the so-called "orb" in a photo looks like it could be caused by your camera flash on a reflective surface, then this is likely the case. By examining this idea first, and not assuming that it must be a ghost because the location where the photo was taken is supposed to be haunted, you will save yourself embarrassment in the future.

This book is not all about fancy cameras and expensive film. It's often about the basic rules of investigation. No matter what sort of camera you might use, or what sort of film you captured your anomalous photo with, it's more about what to do with that photo once you have it. Paranormal research is finally getting to the point that it can be seen as plausible to the public at large. What we have to do is to make a concerted effort to display the best information and evidence that we have (which is often in the form of photographs) and to make sure that those materials have been carefully scrutinized before being presented. Who cares if we are criticized for being too cautious? It is better to be too careful than to make mistakes that can harm the credibility that is so desperately needed in this field.

Let me make one final note in this introduction however --- I do not claim to be an expert on spirit photography. As with all aspects of paranormal research, there are no "experts", no matter who claims to be one. No one has all of the answers when it comes to spirit photography. There is no way to anticipate all of the questions that will come up with paranormal photos or even offer a ready solution to the mysteries that appear. I have written many times before that I am a "skeptic" when it comes to ghosts and especially to paranormal photographs. However, I like to think of myself in the true definition of the word "skeptic", which is someone with an open mind. When it comes to the paranormal, I usually refer to myself as being "optimistically skeptical" in that I am a believer in ghosts but cautious of most of the information that I see and hear. With paranormal photographs (as with haunted houses), I work to rule out every natural cause for the anomalous image in the print before I even consider the idea that it might be a ghost.

For this I am considered an enemy to some and am criticized by many, but I just can't seem to find fault in believing through evidence. As I often quote from Sir Arthur Conan Doyle and his legendary detective, Sherlock Holmes, "Eliminate the impossible and whatever remains, however improbable, must be the truth." Such a statement is never truer than when it pertains to paranormal photographs. We can't be afraid to try and debunk our own photos for this is much better than having someone else do it for us in the future.

So, let me say once more that I am no expert on paranormal photographs. All that I have tried to do with this manual is to take my own experience with these elusive snapshots, based on many years of examining them, and to try and compile some procedures and techniques that may eliminate some of the questions that arise from them. I hope that it turns out to be useful because my goal with this book is simply to provide the reader with some of the essential information needed to create and consider authentic spirit photographs. Hopefully this will help to make your efforts worthwhile and will show you that spirit photography can be both exciting and educational. If I have done my job correctly, you will be able to pick up this book again and again and the ideas and theories here will help you to devise your own theories on ghosts, photography and ghost research in general. As stated already, I won't have all of the answers that you might be seeking but I will pass on my own knowledge gained from past experiences in the field. Good luck and happy hunting!

Troy Taylor
Autumn 2005

1. CAPTURING THE LIGHT

The History of Photography & How the Camera Actually Works

Since the beginning of recorded time, man has created images of the things that surrounded him. In the earliest times, cave dwellers rendered likenesses of animals on the walls of their shelters. Ancient people crafted images on pottery and stone and the Middle Ages saw the birth of thousands of pieces of classic artwork. The eighteenth century saw a demand appear for pictures of people that were less expensive than the formal oil paintings that were commissioned by wealthier patrons. Those of the middle class were able to obtain miniature paintings that were mostly silhouettes, created by a shadow cast from a lamp and then cut free hand by the artist from black paper. These shadow portraits were one-of-a-kind originals until 1786, when a device called a Physionotrace made it possible to make multiple images. When the pointer of it was traced over the lamp created profile, a system of levers caused an engraving tool to reproduce the outline on a copper plate. Details, features and clothing could also be added and then the plate was inked and printed to make as many copies as needed. Soon artists and inventors began to speculate that there might be an optical device created that could produce the images directly.

An optical device like this, known as the camera obscura, was known in ancient times but there was no way to permanently record the images it obtained. Leonardo Da Vinci noted about the camera obscura: "When the images of illuminated objects pass through a small round hole into a very dark room… you will see on paper all those objects in their natural shapes and colours. They will be reproduced in size, and upside down, owing to the intersection of the rays at the aperture."

Various portable models of the camera obscura were invented and in 1589, Giovanni Battista della Porta made note of using a lens rather than a hole to show the images. About 1665, Robert Boyle constructed a model that was the size of a small box and added a lens that could be extended or shortened like a telescope. This way, the image could be shown on a piece of paper placed across the back of the box and directly across from the lens. Scientists began using the camera obscura for solar observations and artists adapted it as an aid in drawing since they could easily trace the projected image.

Around 1800, the first experiments were conducted to try and "fix" the camera obscura images. They were carried out in England by Thomas Wedgwood, who tried to copy paintings that were done on glass onto sheets of paper that were treated with silver nitrate. Unfortunately, the dark images were not permanent and because of their sensitivity to the light, could only be viewed by candlelight.

The first permanent images created by light were produced by a French inventor named Joseph Nicephore Niepce, who was also an amateur artist. He wanted to create a new printmaking technique of lithography but was not very skilled at drawing. He sought ways of transferring images directly onto the printing plate and even tried Wedgwood's methods but also found that the faint, disappearing images created a problem. Over time, Niepce discovered a varnish that was sensitive to light, remaining soft where protected from light and hardening wherever exposed. A plate coated with varnish and exposed by passing light through a drawing or print made on translucent paper could then be washed with a solvent that dissolved the soft areas and left a permanent image on the plate. These first "heliographs" came about in 1822 and Niepce continued working with them for five years before using a camera obscura to record an image on a coated pewter plate. This view was made from the window of his home and required an eight-hour exposure. It is regarded today as the "oldest surviving image produced by a camera."

In 1835, William Henry Fox Talbot discovered the fundamental principle on which modern photography is based ---- the photographic negative from which many copies can be made. He also identified silver chloride as the silver compound that is most suitable for photographic prints. In 1840, he gave the name "calotype" to his improved process in which a latent image could be developed onto paper. Unfortunately though, his work at that time was being overshadowed by a French process that produced a very different photographic image known as the daguerreotype.

THE DAGUERREOTYPE

In January 1837, the discovery was announced of the world's first practical photographic process. The inventor was a man named Louis Daguerre, an artist who was known for his exquisite paintings of dioramas. Through that work, he became familiar with the camera obscura and soon became obsessed with the possibility of fixing the image that the device projected. His early experiments were not successful, but in his quest, he learned of the experiments being done by Joseph Niepce and the two began corresponding and eventually became partners. Niepce died in 1833 and two years later, his son, Isidore, signed an agreement that recognized the technical developments that Daguerre had made in the partnership. He also signed another paper that stated that Daguerre had developed a successful method that produced permanent images and that it was sufficiently different from the one devised by his father that the new process should bear Daguerre's name.

A famous Daguerreotype of a young Abraham Lincoln
(Library of Congress Collection)

Using these statements, Daguerre sold his process to the French government and obtained two substantial lifetime pensions for himself and for Isidore Niepce. Daguerre, however, promoted his invention, organizing public demonstrations of it, circulating a handbook, presenting Daguerreotypes to notables and entering into negotiations with potential commercial agents like Samuel Morse, the inventor of the telegraph and the man who introduced Daguerre's process to Americans.

Despite the fact that the creation of the process was a landmark achievement, it had both advantages and drawbacks. The biggest problem was that to expose and process a Daguerreotype plate, a lot of apparatus and work was required. First, the plate had to be placed in a hand vise and polished with a leather buff, using powdered pumice stone and olive oil. It was finished to a high polish and then placed in a box that had two compartments for iodine crystals and bromide water. The developer then had to watch the plate carefully and estimate when the desired degree of sensitivity had been reached. The prepared plate, loaded into a plate holder, was then placed in the camera, which consisted of two wooden boxes, one of which contained the lens and the other the focusing screen and holder for the plate. After the plate was exposed, which took about 30 seconds, it was removed and taken to the darkroom, where it was placed facedown in the top of the developing box. In the bottom was a dish of mercury, heated by a lamp. As the mercury vapor developed the image, the process could be seen by candlelight through a yellow glass window in the box. When fully developed, the image was then fixed by a chemical treatment that removed the unused silver salts. The plate was then placed on a level stand so that it remained completely horizontal, then covered with a gold-bearing solution and heated. Finally, after it was washed and dried, the finished plate was covered with a decorated covering and a piece of protective glass and then sealed in a brass or foil frame. It had to be an airtight frame for the silver plate would tarnish rapidly if it was exposed to air.

As the reader can see, working with Daguerreotypes was high maintenance work and very expensive and complicated. The work was so cumbersome that a photographer literally had to travel with a small laboratory that limited him to producing fragile, one-of-a-kind pictures that were "direct positives", or mirror-imaged. In the portraits, the faces of the sitters were flattened in a way that made them look "seeming in agony". So not only were they a burden to work with but Daguerreotypes were not exactly the most flattering to those who paid to have them created.

There were improvements to come, however. Exposure times, which were sometimes as long as 30 minutes and did nothing to improve the facial expressions of the sitters, were reduced and the cameras were improved in many ways. Some problems simply could not be solved, such as the highly reflective silver surface. The portraits were described as a "mirror with memory" and the image had the quality of appearing as either a positive or a negative depending on the angle from which it was viewed.

Even with all of the disadvantages, Daguerreotypes captured the popular imagination. It was said that when the artist Paul Deloroche heard about the new process, he exclaimed that "from today, painting is dead". And so, even though the daguerreotyping process was hazardous to the health, thanks to incidents of mercury poisoning, would-be photographers flocked to the process.

The Daguerreotype flourished. In March 1840, Alexander Wolcott and John Johnson, associates of Samuel Morse, opened the first portrait studio in the United States. The process caught on and soon attendance at the Daguerreotype portrait studio became essential in the social circles of the fashion conscious.

By 1844, the Daguerreotype process was virtually perfected, but even so, it was never meant to last. By the middle 1850's, a new photographic process, called the collodion or "wet plate" method, began to overshadow the Daguerreotype and it lasted for several years in America.

THE AMBROTYPE

Prior to the popularity of the Daguerreotype, William Henry Fox Talbot began working with paper negatives that were actually superior to the silver plates. The paper negatives offered the advantages of easy duplication but never had the clarity of detail that could be found in Daguerreotypes. Experimenters tried using glass as a base for light-sensitive compounds but there was a problem with keeping the chemical solutions on the plate as it was being exposed. In 1847, Abel Niepce de Saint-Victor, a cousin of the photography pioneer Niepce, used potassium iodide mixed with egg white to coat the glass. When dry, the plates were sensitized with silver nitrate solution and, after exposure, developed with gallic acid.

An Ambrotype of a Civil War soldier. These photos were relatively inexpensive and held great appeal for enlisted men. (Library of Congress Collection)

In 1851, Frederick Scott Archer tried a different approach, using a clear liquid called collodion to coat the plate. The glue-like substance was a syrupy solution that was made by dissolving nitrocellulose in alcohol and ether. After covering the plate in collodion, it was then dipped in silver nitrate. This rendered the plate light sensitive as long as it remained wet. This was the beginning of the "wet plate" process, which permanently changed photography.

In 1852, Archer described a process in which a solution of mercury bromide was used to whiten the collodion negative. Backing the image with black paper, it caused the negative to appear as a positive. This collodion positive, which looked just like a standard portrait, was soon to replace the Daguerreotype as the portrait of choice. Unlike Daguerreotypes, Ambrotypes, as they came to be called, required little skill and only a small investment. The difference in cost was so great that even the poor could be tempted into the studio for only a few pennies

Archer lived long enough to see his process revolutionize the field but since he published his work freely, he never profited from it and died penniless in 1857.

While the Ambrotypes had many advantages over the Daguerreotypes, there were problems as well. Like the Daguerreotype, each Ambrotype was a one-of-a-kind image. If the subject desired an additional picture, he had to sit for another exposure or have his original copied. Because the image was quite fragile, the collodion positive had to be carefully packaged. It had to be fitted with a brass covering and then covered with glass, followed by a brass rim called a "preserver". The package was then placed in a folding case that would protect it from damage.

The popularity of the Ambrotype was sudden and far-reaching, lasting from the middle 1850's and into the early 1860's. Many Civil War soldiers chose this inexpensive process to immortalize themselves for their loved ones back home. But the process was not meant to last and was soon replaced by another type of collodion positive method that gained its greatest fame during the Civil War.

TINTYPES

The Tintype came about in the latter part of the 1850's but did not become popular for several years afterward. Like the Ambrotype, the Tintype used the same type of collodion, wet plate process but in this case, the process utilized a thin sheet of blackened iron. Named the "melainotype", which combined the Greek words for "black" and "iron", it was soon nicknamed the "Tintype" instead.

The process was patented in 1856 by Hamilton Smith, an Ohio chemistry professor, who then sold the rights to Peter Neff. The Tintype entered the popular consciousness around 1860 and Neff began selling the process all over the country.

While Tintypes lasted well into the Twentieth Century, when they were produced by the gelatin-silver bromide process, early Tintypes were made by the collodion wet plate method. The thin iron plate that was used was coated with a black varnish and then cut to size to be inserted into the camera. It was then exposed in a camera that was often designed to permit all of the chemical operations to be conducted inside of the camera itself. To prevent damage, the exposed plates were then given a protective coat of clear varnish.

This tintype "ghost photo" was not meant to be taken seriously but rather was a comical look at a ghost. Note that the subject is having a "hair raising" experience!

Unlike the Ambrotype, the Tintype was developed as a positive image and so it did not have to be backed or even mounted in an elaborate matter that would allow the image to be clearly seen. The metal base was also less fragile, which is the reason that so many Tintype images have survived into the modern era. Another advantage was that even though the Tintype was also a one-of-a-kind photograph, multiple identical images could be created with a multiple lens camera. They were capable of exposing four, six or even more photographs simultaneously on a single plate. After processing, the duplicate pictures were then snipped apart with metal cutting shears.

Although the Tintype photograph lacked the tonal range of the Ambrotype, its relative inexpensiveness made it very popular, especially in America. The low cost also appealed to soldiers during the war, especially the lower paid Union enlisted men. Confederate Tintypes became progressively less common though, thanks to wartime shortages of sheet metal.

This practical and profitable method of photography continued to be in use, despite the clamor for paper prints, for decades. The process even remained in use, generally at beaches and fairgrounds, until after the days of World War II.

GLASS NEGATIVES & PAPER PRINTS

Even though multiple lens cameras could be used to produce identical images, photography still needed a way to make duplicates on such a practical and inexpensive medium like paper. The "calotypes" created by William Henry Fox Talbot represented an early answer to these needs. Based on experiments that started in 1834, Talbot discovered several basic principles on which modern photography is based, including the use of silver chloride in making prints on paper and the concept of the photographic negative. He began making successful camera pictures but encountered problems with lengthy exposure times and was unable to "fix" the prints to the paper.

Becoming involved with other projects, he neglected his new process for a few years and it was not until he received the shocking news of Daguerre's discovery in 1839 that he picked up where he left off. He returned to his work with renewed energy and, in 1840, discovered that a briefly exposed image, no matter how faint, could be revealed by chemical development. First, Talbot treated fine quality writing paper first with a solution of silver nitrate and then, when dry, with potassium iodidic solution, forming the light sensitive compound silver iodide in the paper fibers. The paper was then washed and dried again.

When it was required for use, the paper was treated, in dim light, with a fresh solution of gallic acid, silver nitrate and acetic acid. The light sensitive sheet was then placed in the camera and exposed, after which the negative image was enhanced by further treatment with the solution. After washing and drying the sheet, the paper negative was waxed to make it more translucent and then it could be used to make as many positive prints as desired. Paper intended for prints was soaked in a solution of ordinary salt, dried, then sensitized with silver nitrate solution. The dried paper was placed in contact with a negative and exposed to sunlight, then fixed and washed.

Talbot called the new process Calotype but many referred to it as "Talbotype", in honor of its inventor. Because of the use of common salt in the developing process, Calotypes were often nicknamed "salt prints". Talbot applied for a patent in 1841, forcing those who wished to use his process to apply for a license. This added to the disadvantages of the Calotype, which already required longer exposures than Daguerreotypes. Although cheaper and able to produce better images, the Calotype became totally eclipsed by the Daguerreotype. In spite of this, the process was used widely by travelers and others who found it well suited to landscape and architectural photography but it was rarely used for portraits.

Glass negatives eventually replaced the paper Calotype ones. They were produced by the collodion process, like Ambrotypes, except that the final step of backing the negative to convert it to a positive was eliminated. Although the quickest negative system that had yet been devised, it still required seven steps, during which the glass plate had to be kept continuously moist and free from light. The final step was warming the plate until it was dry and, while still warm, coating it with a protective varnish.

The glass negative could be used to make prints on the salted paper used for Calotypes but soon a new process was devised. In this printing process, paper was first coated with albumen into which ammonium chloride had been mixed, then sensitized with silver nitrate. A smooth surface resulted, improving the paper's ability to record fine detail. Albumen printing paper was also less given to fading than the Calotype and it remained in use until about 1895.

In addition, there were also various other non-silver papers that were used from about 1860 to 1890 that produced carbon prints, so named for its black pigment, and "plainotypes", which were obtained using platinum salts. The "cyanotype", or "blueprint" process, was named for the distinctive blue color of the prints but was only used infrequently until the 1890's.

The albumen paper remained the most popular and it was ideally suited to meet the increasing demand that resulted from three particular fashions in photographs: the carte de visite, the cabinet photo and the stereograph.

The Carte de Visite: These small photographic cards created a fad that led to more than 300 to 400 million of them being sold annually in England alone, according to reports from the middle 1860's. They were merely small paper photographs, usually portraits, which were mounted on cards about the size of a calling card, although the photos were much smaller. The images were produced on a single plate and were made from either separate poses or with a multiple lens camera. They were then cut apart and fixed to the cards.

The carte de visite craze developed around 1860 and with it came a desire to collect photographs of notables, as well as those of family and friends. Portraits of Napoleon III were distributed throughout France and portraits of Queen Victoria that were published a year later sent hundreds of thousands of French and English citizens into photographic studios to obtain their own carte de visite portraits. In addition to portraits, carte de visite photographs were made of world landmarks, city scenes and historic events. In America, photos of Abraham Lincoln, Kit Carson, Mark Twain and historic figures of the Civil War came to be valuable.

Front and back examples of a common Carte de Visite photograph of the 1880's. The front side featured the subject of the portrait and the back was usually reserved as advertising for the photographic company that produced the cards.

The Cabinet Photograph: While the carte de visite photographs remained in use well into the Twentieth Century and was common in America into the 1880's, their popularity began to diminish in favor of the larger "cabinet" photograph. Introduced in 1866, the paper print photograph was usually about four inches wide, about five and a half inches long and was mounted on a slightly larger card.

Because of its larger size, the cabinet photo was more suitable for serious and formal portraits and soon albums were sold to accommodate the photos of this type. They can frequently be found in antique stores today, often still filled with fading old cabinet photos.

The Stereograph: Another kind of glass negative paper print photograph that enjoyed great popularity during the Nineteenth Century was the stereograph. Also called "stereo views", they were double picture photographs made from slightly different angles that, when viewed through an optical device called a stereoscope, created the illusion of depth.

Originally created back in 1838, stereographs could be found in almost any photographic process but it was not until paper prints became common that the reflective problems caused by Daguerreotypes and the like were eliminated. The viewing of these three-dimensional pictures was very popular from the early 1850's into the late 1870's, then fell from favor before enjoying a resurgence in popularity from about 1887 to the 1930's.

The cards and the viewers remain popular collector's items for history buffs and antique collectors today and the effect created by the dual images still manages to create a thrill for the viewer, especially when looking back on long forgotten, historic scenes.

Stereoscopic pictures and the viewers required to see them properly remain popular today as collector's items for photography and antique buffs. I have dozens of them in my own collection.

DRY PLATES AND SNAPSHOTS

As successful as the wet plate process was, there was still a need for a process during which a prepared plate could be kept for some time before being exposed to the camera. There were many early attempts to keep the plates wet for extended periods but all of them failed until 1855, when J.N. Taupenot devised the first successful "dry plate" method. He did it using sensitized layers of collodion and albumen, which allowed the plates to be stored for weeks before exposure.

In 1864, W.B. Bolton and B.J. Sayce discovered that an emulsion of silver bromide in collodion, applied to a glass plate and then allowed to dry, produced a plate with a lengthy shelf life. The only drawback was that the plates were less sensitive than dry plates and required longer exposure times.

A major development was achieved by Dr. Richard Leach Maddox in 1871 when he returned to a substance that was earlier used in photography --- gelatin. He found that a mixture of silver nitrate and cadmium bromide in a solution of warm gelatin yielded a silver bromide emulsion that produced effective dry plates.

Two years later, John Burgess began to sell an already mixed gelatin emulsion for coating glass plates and the following year, another inventor, Richard Kennett, marketed the emulsion in a dried form that could be mixed with water before use. Called "Kennett's Patented Sensitized Pellicle", it inadvertently gained sensitivity from the heat-drying process by which the gelatin "pellicle" was prepared. This created the most sensitive plate so far but it remained for Charles Bennett to investigate the increased sensitivity and to use prolonged heating to develop both highly sensitive plates and ones that were easily manufactured as well. The new process was successful and by 1880, photographers could travel without the dark tent and wagon full of chemicals that were previously required. Now, he could make an excursion with just his camera and tripod and a few plate holders loaded with prepared dry plates. They could later be processed on the photographer's return to his studio. Remaining popular until the 1920's, the gelatin dry plate glass negatives brought several important changes to photography, especially the means to measure sensitivity of the plate. This was notable since, unlike the wet plates (which were developed in the field and permitted the photographer to make successively corrected exposures) the results of dry plate photography were not immediately apparent.

Along with plates for which the sensitivity could be measured came methods of calculating the necessary lens aperture and exposure time. By 1886, this was accomplished by pocket watch size devices that were used until the 1920's. With the reduction of exposure times, which were accomplished by increasing the aperture of the lens, came radical advancements in photography. For the first time, photographs could be achieved that required exposures of fractions of seconds and the photography of moving subjects became practicable at last.

Because of the lengthy exposure times needed by the earlier photographic plates, any movement produced a blur. For this reason, not only were photos of moving people or objects out of the question, but even those who sat for portraits had to have their heads held by clamps that had to be fixed to the back of chairs. This is the reason why you never see any sort of photos from the Civil War era that are anything other than posed portraits or still landscapes.

Shuttered cameras first came into use with stereographs and were made possible by the small images that were produced. When stereo views were made of scenes involving movement, both pictures had to be exposed at precisely the same instant. In that way, simple shutters, consisting of flaps or sliding plates, could create exposures as brief as one-fourth of a second.

The instantaneous photo was characterized as a "snapshot" (a term applied to a hurriedly aimed shot) by Sir John Herschel in 1860. Such brief exposures permitted cameras to be freed from the tripod, which had been used by the photographer to prevent movement and then blurring of the picture. Now, with the addition of a viewfinder to aid in the framing of the photo, cameras could be handheld. In 1881, Thomas Bola called his small, box-type camera a "Detective" camera, and soon diminutive models were hidden in bags, hats and even in the handle of walking sticks. The glass plates remained a problem though, thanks to rather awkward mechanisms that held several dry plates at once. Such cameras came to be known as "magazine" cameras and became the forerunner to a revolutionary development in America that allowed successive snapshots to be made quickly.

THE KODAK & ROLL FILM

The dry photo process that had been devised by Charles Bennett gained the attention of an American named George Eastman. The Rochester, New York bank clerk turned amateur photographer was so impressed with the plates that he began manufacturing gelatin dry plates and selling them through a photographic supply house as early as 1880. He became the first person to do so in the United States.

Eastman soon sought additional ways to simplify photography, realizing that the complexity of it, along with the messy processes, was keeping it from being enjoyed by everyday people. Working with camera manufacturer William H. Walker, Eastman developed a holder for a lengthy roll of paper negative "film". Although there had been earlier experiments with such things, the Eastman-Walker invention combined a roll-holding feature with very sensitive, lightweight material. It became an immediate success.

Soon after, Eastman designed a small, hand-held camera that utilized the roll holder. Patented in 1886 with an employee named F.M. Cossitt, the small model was produced with a run of only 50 cameras. Too complicated and too expensive to do well, the entire lot was sold off to a dealer the following year. Two years later, in 1888, Eastman developed a new model that was made up of a small box that contained a roll of paper-based film that was sufficient for about 100 exposures. It was simple to operate but the photographer had to keep track of the pictures for there was no exposure counter. Eastman gave his camera the invented name of "Kodak", which he felt gave it a firm, uncompromising moniker.

Although there had been earlier roll-film cameras, the Kodak was the first to be backed up by a service that processed the exposed pictures. Realizing that most people did not have the time, skill or inclination to develop their own film, Eastman adopted the slogan "You Press the Button, We Do the Rest". After completing the roll, the customer sent the camera to Eastman's factory in New York, where the film was unloaded, developed and printed. After that, a reloaded camera was shipped back to the owner, along with the processed prints. After much success, Eastman introduced a new camera in 1889 with an improved shutter. He called this one the No. 2 Kodak.

At the end of that year, Eastman also introduced a new product that replaced the old paper-based film, which was complicated to handle since it required the processed negative image to be stripped from the paper base before printing. The new product was a roll film on a celluloid base and with this clear, flexible material, the roll-film camera finally became practical.

PHOTOGRAPHY FOR THE MASSES

The Kodak camera and the development of celluloid roll film launched the heyday of popular snapshot photography, although it took years to solve all of the problems that remained. The need to expose a hundred images, for example, was solved by shorter films and simpler methods of loading that did not involve sending the camera back to the factory. In fact, by 1891, cameras had been devised that even allowed the film to be loaded in daylight. Numbered markings were placed on the black backing paper that helped protect the celluloid film from light when it was wound on a spool. These numbers could be read through a window on the camera's back and they permitted the film to be wound a precise distance each time until a new number was centered in the window. Eastman incorporated the idea in his pocket Kodak of 1895 and the first of his folding Kodak cameras in 1897.

An ad for the Eastman Kodak Brownie from the Youth's Companion 1900. This was the camera that truly brought photography to the masses

Despite all of this, Eastman still felt that photography was too expensive for the masses and he assigned his camera designer, Frank Brownell, to develop a simple camera that could be cheaply reproduced. The result was the Brownie Kodak, which was introduced in February 1900. Even though most assumed that the name for the camera came from its creator, Frank Brownell, the designation was actually supposed to have been sparked by the popularity of the Brownies, the little fairies in Palmer Cox's children's stories. This was tied to Eastman's advertising strategy that stated that the Brownie camera had a "simple Kodak method that enables even a child to make successful and charming photographs."

The Brownie captured the imagination of the public but not everyone was pleased with the popular revolution in photography. According to one newspaper report, "Several decent young men are forming a Vigilance Committee for the purpose of thrashing the cads with cameras who go about seaside places taking snapshots of ladies emerging from the deep."

Regardless, photographic enthusiasm continued to spread and further advancements were made. In 1893, the first practical motion pictures were made using Eastman's film and were shown on Thomas Edison's Kinetoscope viewing machine. The motion pictures were based on earlier experiments conducted by Edward Muybridge in 1878. He had arranged a series of cameras with shutters that were triggered by trip wires across the path of a galloping horse. This produced a picture sequence that showed the horse in motion. The 1893 images, shown at the Columbian Exposition in Chicago, were the first to show motion using a steady roll of film.

More significant steps in photography followed. One of the most important was the development of the camera flash. Although flash powder had been used for illumination of subjects almost from the beginning of snapshot photography, it was, not surprisingly, very dangerous. The flashbulb was invented in the 1920's and automatically triggered flashes came with professional cameras in the middle 1930's. The first simple flash camera, the Falcon Press Flash, came along in 1939.

Another development came in 1938, when the first fully automatic camera was developed. It used a photoelectric cell to move a meter needle, which was locked in place by the initial pressure on the shutter release. Then, a spring loaded sensor linked to the aperture setting moved until it was stopped by a locked needle, automatically setting the exposure.

Among the most important developments in the field was the introduction of color photography. Although its possibilities were considered early in the history of photography, the earliest color pictures were nothing more than black and white Daguerreotypes that were hand colored. The first color photograph was produced as early as 1861 by James Clerk Maxwell, but the first color plates were not produced until 1896. The first genuinely successful plates however were marketed by the Lumiere Brothers in 1907 and were called Autochrome plates. They ceased making them in 1932 but three color "carbro" plates began to be used by fashion photographers in the 1930's. However, in 1935, the great breakthrough in color photography came with the introduction of Kodachrome film.

Kodachrome was produced at the suggestion of two musicians, Leopold Godowsky Jr. and Leopold Mannes. They proposed coating film with three different black and white emulsions, each sensitive to one of the primary colors of light. A single exposure, when processed, produced three superimposed images, each of which could be selectively dyed to yield a full color picture. Kodachrome was initially introduced as a motion picture film but a version for still cameras was soon created.

About that same time, Agfa, in Germany, produced a film that used the same three layers (sensitive to red, blue and green light) but the color-forming compounds were placed directly into the film's emulsion. The Agfa and Kodachrome systems are the basis for almost all color photography that is in use today.

More later improvements in photography involved cameras that had "instant" features. The Polaroid Land Camera was marketed starting in 1948. Within a minute of being removed from the camera, the print yielded a sepia-toned image. It was a huge success and many improved cameras and film followed, including Polaroid color film in 1963. The Kodak Pocket Instamatic later simplified a common problem for the average person who wanted to dabble in photography: loading the film. The Instamatic came about in 1963 and was similar to the Brownie but introduced simple load-in cartridges that could be dropped in only one way. In 1982, Kodak also introduced the so-called Disc Camera that had cartridges in the form of a circular disc that contained the negatives. But the small size of the negatives resulted in grainy images and the camera failed to interest the public in the way the Instamatic had. One of the most popular types of cameras in recent years have been the APS cameras that featured the simple drop-in cartridges and also allow the photographer to photograph at various sizes, including classic size and wide panoramic prints.

DIGITAL CAMERAS

The origins of digital cameras can be linked back to the computer imaging that was being done by NASA back in the 1960's. During this time, NASA was preparing for the Apollo Lunar Exploration missions and in advance of men landing on the moon, they sent out a series of probes to map the surface. The probes relied on video cameras that were outfitted with transmitters that could broadcast analog signals back to mission control. The weak transmissions were often plagued by natural interference and television at that time could not transform them into images that were coherent.

NASA researchers soon began searching for ways to enhance the signals by processing them through computers. The signals were analyzed by the computer and then converted into digital information. The interference was removed and the critical data could be enhanced to produce clear images of the moon. This was the first real digital imaging to be done but it would soon revolutionize photography as we know it.

Digital technology was not only used by NASA to explore the solar system but it also created a number of medical imaging devices, changed the world of entertainment and made photography and video accessible to people who had never used it before.

The digital cameras of today capture images electronically and convert them into digital data that can be stored on a chip inside of the camera. The images can then be transferred and manipulated using a computer. Like conventional cameras, digital devices have a lens, a shutter and an aperture but they do not use film. When light passes through the lens, it is directed to the a light sensitive chip called a "charged coupling device" (CCD). The CCD converts the light into electrical impulses, feeds it into the processing chip and then transforms that into digital information. Digital images offer many things that a standard camera cannot, freeing the photographer from film and optics and allowing the images captured to be transformed in ways that have never been available before.

All images that are seen by the human eye are formed from energy given off by light. In order for the digital camera to store an optical image, it must be converted into digital information. A simple photograph is composed of a wide range of color and light variations and like the spectrum of natural light that it represents, the tones of the photo are continuous and unbroken. However, a digital image consists of scores of points of light that have been sampled from the light spectrum. The range of tone is determined by the camera's capacity to store and sample different light values. The more expensive the camera, or at least the greater number of megapixels of light that it offers, the better image the photographer will obtain. When a photo is taken, the pixels in the image are assigned a placed on the color scale that corresponds to its place and value in the optical image. The more pixels, the greater the range of tone for the image. Once the camera has determined the proper colors and tone, the CCD calculates a sampling rate for the entire image.

Most digital images form within a fraction of a second and in that instant, an image made of light is transformed into a stream of numerical data that can be changed and altered to look just like anything that the creative photographer wants. There is no question that digital cameras have permanently changed the world of photography--- whether it be the photography of the mundane or that of the spirit world.

CAMERAS & FILM

After learning all (and more) than he or she can possibly need to know about the history of photography, the reader has to wonder how all of this information can pertain to the use of their own modern camera. Surprisingly, this information is actually very relevant because in order to properly use a camera in paranormal research, the operator needs to know just how that camera operates --- and also how different this device is from the human eye. Many have written about "seeing the world through the camera lens", perhaps never realizing how radically different it is to actually see something rather than to capture it with a camera.

The human eye does work in some ways like the shutter of the camera. It opens and closes in a blink or can be closed at the speed of a long exposure. The lens of the human eye works to focus on what it is looking at in the same way that the focus ring on a camera can be used. The human eye does this by reflex but the camera has to be manually focused, either by hand or by the camera's inner workings. The iris of the eye dilates to let in more or less light in the same way that the f-stop on a camera does. The retina of the eye receives and image and imprints it on the consciousness in the same way that images are captured on the camera's film. At that point though, the comparison between the two comes to an end. The images that we see with our eyes are collected and analyzed by our brain and anything that we see is subject to adaptation and censorship by our personality. Images that are collected by the camera are captured just as they are and are not distorted by emotion or disbelief, freezing a moment of time and space in a way that our eyes cannot do. Could this be why, as some believe, that ghosts can be captured with a camera but sometimes are not seen by the human eye?

That is a question that we will de delving into more deeply in the chapters that follow but first, we will take a look at some of the basic operations of the modern camera.

As the reader has already learned in the previous pages, the camera basically consists of two things: a box that is tight enough to keep out light and a lens. The lens collects the light from the object that is being photographed and focuses on the image. The box is sealed so that it does not take in any other light than what is coming in through the lens. Beyond that, cameras are also equipped with a shutter, a simple timing device that restricts the length of time that light is allowed to reach the film, and an aperture, which is a hole that is located just behind the lens. The aperture is opened wider or smaller to brighten the image. This is known as the f-stop and the larger the number, the smaller the aperture. A higher number allows more light than a smaller number f-stop. All of these items can be adjusted with manual cameras, although today, most cameras are automatic and these settings are handled by the mechanism of the camera itself.

These Single Reflex Cameras (or SLR cameras) are the most commonly used devices for photographers and ghost hunters alike. A single lens handles the viewing and the taking of the picture but this type of device also allows manual focusing and changes in f-stop settings, exposure settings and more. They can be a little more complicated for the amateur but are well worth the trouble of learning to use them. Many others prefer the simple "point and shoot" type cameras, which are very simple to use and which handle all of the settings automatically. Which is better?

Many people have asked me to recommend various types of cameras and film over the years and later in the book, I will offer some suggestions. However,

I can say honestly that I have seen remarkable photos that have been taken with everything from expensive SLR cameras to instant cameras to even cheap, disposable cameras. The main thing to remember is that it's not the camera that's most important, but rather the person behind the lens.

But how do we "capture the light", so to speak and make the camera work?

The light around us can be thought of as rays of energy that emanate from or reflect off of every point of an object and travel from it in straight lines. These lines travel randomly, so the lens of the camera serves to control their progress. The curved lens collects and redirects the light, bending it as it does so. The thicker and more curved the lens is, the greater its ability is to bend the light and the more the light is bent, the shorter the focal length will be. When the lens is focused at infinity, it is one focal length away from the "focal plane", where an image is actually formed. The operation of focusing the lens, whether done manually or automatically, brings the lens away from the focal plane and brings nearer objects into focus. When the lens is focused on a point a certain distance away, there will be an area in front of and behind this point that appears very sharp on film. This is referred to as "depth of field". Using the depth of field can be helpful to the photographer and not just to create better looking pictures. One way that it's useful is allowing the photographer to focus the camera in advance of taking photos during times when there may not be time to manually focus an SLR camera.

The light captured by the camera is also connected to the camera's shutter, which has been mentioned previously. The shutter allows light to reach the camera by opening and closing at various speeds, from very fast to very slow. Using a fast shutter and a high speed film, the photographer can literally freeze even fast moving objects and also take pictures under very low light conditions.

Which brings us to the film used for cameras. The early portion of this chapter detailed the progress made from photographic plates to rolled film but not everyone understands the various speeds of film and how it can best be used. Some of the most important questions involve the best kinds of film to use and what speed that film should be. For the most part, I always recommend that photographers use a well-known brand name film that they can be sure is not out of date. Like food, film also has an expiration date and it's best to check for this before buying it. If the film is outdated, it may not work properly and the user will be very disappointed if it fails to develop correctly.

When it comes to the best speed of film to use, that answer largely depends on how, when and under what conditions your plan to use it. Whether the film is being used indoors, outdoors under lighted conditions, in low light or even in total darkness all factor into what speed of film the photographer should be using. The smaller the number of film, like ASA 100, the slower the film speed is and the longer the shutter will have to be left open in order for it to gather sufficient light and gain the proper exposure. However, the benefit to a slower speed film is that it has a smaller grain and it makes the picture quality better and allows for better enlargements of the print. The drawback though, especially to those who plan to use the film for paranormal research, is that slow speed films are difficult to use indoors and almost impossible to use in the dark.

If the user plans to shoot photos in the dark, or even inside of a building in dim or ambient light, it is recommended to use a faster film, such as ASA 400 or above. These higher speed films gather the available light much quicker and will also allow the user to disable their automatic flash and to shorten the exposure time for their photos. However, the grain of such films is much larger, so enlargements will be limited and the quality of the prints will be poorer than with lower speed films. However, a faster speed film does have definite advantages, especially when used for paranormal research. It allows for a faster shutter speed and a smaller aperture to be used, which generally makes taking photos simpler. As mentioned though, the faster the speed, the coarser the film grain. No matter what quality brand of film is used, there are simply more individual silver halide grains in the emulsion of faster films. The exposure, as well as the degree and type of development, cause the clumping together of these grains and this becomes obvious in the print as a grainy, spotted effect. The only way to stop this is to use a slower film, which can often be detrimental to low light photography. Most photographers simply choose to use a faster film because they can handle both underexposure and overexposure and still yield acceptable prints. They are best suited for fast shutter speeds and under darkened conditions, when paranormal researchers take the most photographs.

The other choice for film that can be used in dark conditions is an infrared film, which can be difficult to work with to say the least. Later in the book, we'll take a closer look at the best ways to use this type of film, and others, in paranormal research.

With our primer on the history of photography, and the basic operations of cameras and film completed, we can begin to take a look at the "other" side of photography, a side that is totally ignored by most scholars and experts in the field --- the capturing of the spirit world on film.

2. PHOTOGRAPHING THE UNSEEN

The Mysterious History of Spirit Photography

Most of mankind's supernormal talents are by definition non-physical and so are difficult to demonstrate, but the end product of supernormal photography is a physical record that cannot be denied.

Cyril Permutt

Spirit photography is nearly as old as photography itself but when the first photographers found inexplicable images in their work, they assumed they were caused by unknown variables in the strange chemicals and new apparatus they were using. At the dawn of photography, it was nearly impossible to take pictures of people. With the exposure times of a half hour or more needed to impress an image on the paper films and coated plates of the day, it was impractical to expect anyone to sit still for so long. It was not until improvements came along in cameras, lenses, photographic chemicals and processes that exposure times were reduced to a matter of seconds instead of dozens of minutes. By this time, people were flocking to the portrait studios to have their images immortalized in time.

Interest in the Spiritualist movement had been on the rise since the announcement of spirit rappings at the home of the Fox family of New York in 1848. Of course, no photographs were taken of the weird events at the Fox home because indoor photography was impossible for a number of years afterward. But the days of spirit photography were coming....

In those days, the photographer had to first prepare a plate by coating it with collodion, bathing it in silver nitrate and then taking the photo while the plate was still wet. Each new exposure was an exciting event but imagine how excited W. Campbell of Jersey City must have been when he achieved what is considered to be the first spirit photograph. At the *American Photographic Society* meeting of 1860, he displayed a test photograph that he had taken of an empty chair. There had been no one else in the studio at the time but when the plate was developed, it showed the image of a small boy seated in the chair. Campbell was never able to produce any other photographs of this sort and thanks to this, it would not be until the following year that the real history of spirit photography began.

On October 5, 1861, in a photographic studio at 258 Washington Street, a Boston engraver and amateur photographer named William Mumler developed some experimental self-portraits that he had taken and was startled to find that the image of a ghostly young woman appeared in one of the photos with him. He was said to have recognized the young woman as a cousin who had passed away 12 years before. He later recalled that while posing for the portrait, he had experienced a trembling sensation in his right arm that left him particularly exhausted. The photograph attracted great attention and it was examined by not only Spiritualists but by some of the leading photographers of the day. They all came to accept the fact that, as Mumler stated, "This photograph was taken by myself of myself and there was not a living soul in the room besides myself". Mumler was soon overwhelmed by public demand for his photographs and he soon gave up his regular job as an engraver to devote himself entirely to spirit photography.

A Spirit Photograph taken by William Mumler in the late 1860's

William Black, a leading Boston photographer who was known as the inventor of the acid nitrate bath for photographic plates, was one of the professionals who investigated Mumler and his methods. After sitting for Mumler in his studio, Black examined his camera, plate and bath and kept his eye on the plate from the moment its preparations began until it was locked into the camera. After his portrait was taken, Black removed it from the camera and took it into the darkroom himself, where, as it developed, he was stunned to see the image of a man, leaning over his shoulder. Black was convinced that Mumler was the genuine article and could somehow entice the spirits to appear on film.

Others were not so sure. Mumler had never before been interested in the spirits or Spiritualism and his charge of $5 per photograph began to arouse the suspicions of many that he was just in it for the money. He became the object of great controversy and he eventually moved to New York, where he then began charging $10 for photographs. His critics and the disbelievers howled once more. In spite of this, he had many supporters as well. One of them was U.S. Court of Appeals Judge John Edmonds, who had originally come to Mumler's studio convinced the man was a con artist, but left convinced that he could actually conjure up genuine psychic photos. Another famed supporter joined the ranks of some of the most eminent people in the land when she came to Mumler's studio for a photograph of her own. This woman was Mary Todd Lincoln, widow of the slain president, and she became the subject of Mumler's most famous spirit photo, which will be discussed later in the chapter.

In 1863, a Dr. Child of Philadelphia reported that Mumler was willing to allow him to thoroughly investigate the matter of his spirit photos and, as he said, to try and find a rational explanation for the mystery. He permitted Child to watch all of his operations in the darkroom, and out of it, and also allowed him to examine his apparatus. Dr. Child displayed the pictures made at the time, while he and several friends watched the entire process, from the plate cleaning to the fixing. He took the precaution to mark each plate with a diamond before it was used and yet on each one of them was a spirit image. Child had failed completely to discover any human agent that was responsible for the formation of the spirit pictures. Each of them differed considerably from one another and Child could not come up with a way to duplicate them.

However, the "extras", as they came to be called, in Mumler's photographs did not amaze everyone. After much controversy, pressure from city officials led to him being arrested and charged with fraud. But the testimony of a number of leading New York residents, including famed Broadway producer Jeremiah Gurney who affirmed that as a professional photographer he had never seen anything like the images that Mumler produced, led to Mumler being exonerated and his case dismissed.

As it would turn out later though, the courts may have been a little too hasty about dropping all of the charges against Mumler....

According to an article in *Scientific American* magazine in 1902, Mumler may have been more clever than anyone ever gave him credit for --- and a much bigger fraud. Experiments in duplicating spirit photos that came about after the heyday of William Mumler achieved a simple way of creating spectral images that would have passed inspection by those who examined Mumler's plates and apparatus at the time. This method involved making a very thin positive image on glass, the same size as the plate that was to be used in producing the spirit photo. The glass was then placed in the holder where the plate would later be placed as well. With the glass in position, the plate could be inserted under the watchful eye of the examiner and the photograph produced. With the weak positive superimposed, the ghostly image would appear, along with the sitter, on the negative plate. In this way, the plates would never be tampered with and in examinations like those conducted by Dr. Child, his mark would appear on the plate that was used and he would never assume that anything out of the ordinary was taking place.

Could this have been Mumler's secret? If we assume that fraud may have been involved with the creation of his photos, then yes, it could have been. But what about those photos that contained the images of loved ones that Mumler knew nothing about? Could his research have been so thorough that he delved into the private lives --- and photographs --- of those who made appointments so far in advance that he was able to obtain photos of dead relatives that could appear in his spirit photographs? And what of those who came to him without an appointment and yet their loved ones still managed to appear on film? Was it wishful thinking that the extras appeared to be so familiar? Perhaps --- or perhaps not.

A fairly standard spirit photograph of days past. This was taken by William Hope of a Mrs. Longcake and what was alleged to be her deceased sister in law.

Other photographers, both amateur and professional, soon began to appear, eager to capitalize on the success of William Mumler. In America and Great Britain, new studios began to open and the photographers began to call themselves "mediums", claiming the ability to make dead appear in photographs. Spirit photography soon became a popular pastime and literally thousands of dollars were made from those who came to have their portraits taken. One photographer, William Hope, claimed to take more than 2,500 spirit photographs during a period of about two decades.

William Hope was one of the premiere spirit photographers of the era and was considered by believers and supporters to be a true master of the art of producing spirits on ordinary photographic plates. To others, he was a clever trickster and while he had more than his share of detractors, he was often accused of fraud but was never caught at it ---- thanks to the controversy that surrounded the main attempt to expose him.

Hope was born in Crewe, England in 1863 and as a young man, went to work as a carpenter. His talent for capturing the spirits in photographs allegedly came about around 1905 when he and a friend were taking turns photographing one another. In a photo that was taken by Hope, there was an extra and as it turned out, the extra in question was the deceased sister of the photograph's subject.

Not long after this incident, a group of six people organized a Spiritualist hall in Crewe for the purpose of creating spirit photographs. The group became renowned as the "Crewe Circle" with William Hope as its leader. During their early efforts, the circle destroyed all of the negatives of the photos they took for fear of being suspected of witchcraft. However, when Archbishop Thomas Colley, a lifelong enthusiast of both the supernatural and Spiritualism, joined the circle, they began to make their work public.

Ironically, Hope's first brush with exposure as a fraud came when Archbishop Colley arranged his first sitting. According to the story, Hope doctored the photograph with the wrong spirit extra, substituting another elderly woman for Colley's mother. When Hope tried to confess his fraud to Colley, the other man dismissed his confession as "nonsense"--- he would recognize his mother when he saw her and the extra in the photo was certainly his mother, he stated. To prove his case, he even put a notice in the local newspaper and asked that all of those who remembered his mother should call at the rectory. No fewer than 18 people selected Hope's mistake from among several others and said that it definitely showed the ghost of the late Mrs. Colley.

In February 1922, Hope was almost exposed again but this time, the attempt almost backfired on the accuser and there remain some questions about the incident to this day. By that time, Hope had moved to London and had established himself as a professional medium. The Society for Psychical Research (SPR) decided to investigate Hope's claims and sent a new member, Harry Price, to look into it. The young Price had a good working knowledge of conjuring and would later make a name for himself as one of Britain's leading ghost hunters. During the investigation, Price claimed to detect evidence of trickery by Hope but questions immediately arose as to whether it was Price, and not Hope, who had tampered with the photographic plates.

Price told a different story of the incident and blamed his problems with the Spiritualist community on the controversy. Even though he had recently joined the SPR, Price had already exposed a number of fraudulent mediums, earning him the dislike of much of the community. During the sitting, which was organized with hymn singing and prayers like a standard séance, Hope and Price went into the adjoining dark room. Price examined the photographic slide that Hope planned to use and he secretly impressed 12 small punctures into it with a needle. He then was asked to open a packet of plates that he had brought with him. These plates had come from the Imperial Dry Plate Co. and had been imprinted (at Price's suggestion) with their trademark in the corner. The trademark would then appear on the negative of whatever picture was developed.

Price loaded two plates into the slide and then Hope asked for the slide.

As he took it from Price's hand, the investigator watched Hope's movements very carefully, which was hard to do in the dull, red darkness of the room. Very quickly, in one smooth movement, Hope placed the dark slide into the left breast pocket of his coat and then, apparently, pulled it back out again. Price knew that the slide had been changed but sat down for the photograph to be taken anyway. When it was over, he refused to sign the plates, as Hope wanted him to, and as he examined the slide, he discovered that his 12 needle marks had "mysteriously" vanished. It was clearly not the same slide that he had given to Hope to use. He did not accuse Hope of a swindle on the spot, fearing that his evidence of deception would be destroyed, but took away two photographs that had been taken of Price, one of which contained a beautiful female "extra" --- but on neither plate was the Imperial Dry Plate trademark! Hope had managed to switch the plates as well. He was able to show that they were not the same type of plates that he had given to Hope to use, as they were a different thickness, weight and color and were "fast" plates, while the ones that Hope gave back to him were "slow" ones.

In the May issue of the *Journal of the London SPR*, Price published a report about the incident under the title "Cold Light on Spiritualistic Phenomena" and it was later reprinted as a separate booklet. Immediately, he was attacked from the Spiritualist camp. Sir Arthur Conan Doyle, who was a supporter of the Crewe Circle, denounced Price and his methods. He and the Spiritualist newspapers accused Price of trickery and of switching the plates himself in a plan to discredit the medium. Sir Oliver Lodge however, who was a proponent of Spiritualism, believed that Hope was a fraud and wrote to Harry Price saying: "I don't see how your proofs of Hope's duplicity could be more complete."

More than 11 years after this incident, the widow of a man who worked for Hope admitted in an article that after Price's séance, her husband went through Hope's luggage and "found in a suitcase a flash lamp with a bulb attachment, some cut-out photographic heads and some hairs". Unfortunately, these devastating facts were suppressed in 1922 and Price would later comment that if not for this suppression, his entire relationship with Conan Doyle could have been preserved. "This vital information would have ended my controversy with Sir Arthur," he said. "Incidentally, it would have ended Hope too!"

Although Hope certainly had his detractors, he had his supporters too, including Conan Doyle, who wrote his book *The Case for Spirit Photography* in response to the Price incident. He was also supported by eminent scientists Sir William Crookes and Sir William Barrett. Many have suspected that trickery was involved in Crookes' sitting though. The physicist was in his 80's in 1916, when he had his sitting, and had just recently lost his wife. His assistant at the time, J.H. Gardiner, told Crookes' biographer that the negative from which Hope's photograph of Lady Crookes was reproduced showed clear signs of double exposure but that Crookes preferred to ignore this.

However, to make matters more perplexing, not all of the sittings that Hope conducted ended with questionable results. Throughout his career, Hope gained support from many quarters and figured prominently into a book about survival after death by Reverend Charles Tweedale, who owned a haunted house in the town of Otley in Yorkshire. In his writings, Tweedale gives many accounts of Hope's prowess as a spirit photographer, stating that there was no fraud evident in the majority of Hope's cases in which people called upon him unannounced, even with secret identities, and obtained clearly recognizable spirit images. One case was that of Mrs. Hortense Leverson, who came to Hope and was given a psychic photograph of her recently deceased husband, Major Leverson, who had been on the staff of the War Office. She was absolutely convinced that the photograph was legitimate. She, along with dozens (perhaps hundreds) of others, believed that Hope was absolutely genuine.

William Hope died on March 7, 1933, leaving a number of mysteries behind. Was he real -- was he merely a fraud? No one can say for sure and like so many of the other enigmas connected to the practice of spirit photography, this one also remained unsolved.

In many cases though, the answers are not as mysterious. Typically in spirit photographs, ghostly faces materialized, floating above and behind the living subjects. In others, fully formed spirits would appear, usually draped in white sheets. Unfortunately, the methods of producing such images were simple. The fraudulent photographers became adept at doctoring their work, superimposing images on plates with living sitters and adding ghostly apparitions and double exposures. The appearance of the fully formed apparition was even easier. Many cameras demanded that the subject of the photo remain absolutely still, sometimes for periods of up to one minute, all the while, the shutter of the camera remains open. During this time, it was very simple for the photographer's assistant to quietly appear behind the sitter, dressed in appropriate "spirit attire". The assistant remained in place for a few moments and then ducked back out of the photo again. On the finished plate, it would seem that a transparent "figure" had made an appearance. This could be done with cameras that required even an exposure time of a few seconds with an assistant appearing for only a second or two from behind a curtain.

This type of "trick photo" was first mentioned in photography journals in 1856. Ten years later, Sir David Brewster recalled the technique when he saw some of the early spirit photos that were produced. He remembered another photo that he had seen of a young boy who had been sitting on a step near a doorway and who had apparently gotten up and left about halfway through the exposure. As a result, the seated image was transparent in the finished photo. Brewster wrote: "The value and application of this fact did not at first present itself to me, but after I had contrived the lenticular stereoscope I saw that such transparent pictures might be used for the various purposes of entertainment." Ghost and spirit photographs and stereographs were sold commercially in America through the 1860's and 1870's but were nothing more than a parlor novelty and were not meant to be taken as genuine spirit photographs.

Other methods of obtaining fraudulent photographs were used as well. Prepared plates and cut films were often switched and substituted by slight of hand tricks, replacing those provided by the investigator. And while this might have fooled a credulous member of the general public, slight of hand maneuvers and instances of assistants prancing through photos draped in sheets did not convince hardened and skeptical investigators that the work of the spirit photographers was credible or genuine. However, in case after case, investigators walked away stumped as to how the bizarre images managed to appear on film. For every fraud who was exposed, there was at least one other photographer who was never caught cheating. This is what has kept the curiosity of the public about the early spirit photographers after more than a century has gone by.

One of my favorite phony spirit photographs! This photo was taken by Fredrick Hudson. The sitter was Raby Wootton, who, with friends, took the photograph and developed it themselves without allowing Hudson to take part in it. They never realized how easy it would be for Hudson to switch the plate that he gave them to develop!

But unfortunately, there were many who were not so honest. At about the same time that William Mumler was going on trial in New York for fraud, a popular spirit photographer named Frederick Hudson emerged on the scene in London. He was brought to the public's attention by Mrs. Samuel Guppy, a well-known medium of the day. Hudson was eventually investigated by a famous professional photographer named John Beattie in 1873. He carried out a series of experiments with Hudson that were later published in the *British Journal of Photography*. At that time, Hudson was charging a steep fee for his photos, but only with the understanding that he could not be blamed if nothing unusual appeared, which often happened.

In his article, Beattie described how, with a friend, he had examined the glass room in Hudson's garden where the experiments were to take place, the operating and developing room with its yellow light and porcelain baths, the 10 x 8 inch camera with its 6 - inch lens and all of the machinery involved. He also maintained that he had marked the photographic plate to be used and watched it being coated and prepared.

For the first photograph that Hudson took, using an exposure of about one minute, Beattie sat as the subject in profile to the background and Hudson's daughter (acting as the medium) stood next to him. No extra appeared in the photo. For the next experiment, Beattie wrote: "All was the same except that the medium sat behind the background. On the picture being developed, a sitting figure beside myself came out in front of me and between the background and myself. I am sitting in profile in the picture -- the figure is in a three-quarter position -- in front of me, but altogether between me and the background. The figure is draped in black, with a white colored plaid over the head, and is like both a brother and a nephew of mine. This last point I do not press because the face is like that of a dead person and under lighted."

Beattie continued: "In my last trial -- all, if possible, more strictly attended to then before, and in the same place relative to me -- there came out a standing female figure, clothed in black skirt, and having a white-colored, thin linen drapery something like a shawl pattern, upon her shoulders, over which a mass of black hair loosely hung. The figure is in front of me and, as it were, partially between me and the camera."

Beattie had assumed that Hudson was, in some way, faking the photographs but was now no longer convinced of this. He was sure that the figures were not double exposures, had not been projected in some way, and were not the result of mirrors or even the result of images that had been manipulated onto the plates during the developing process.

What he did not take into consideration though was that the images could have been on the plates all along -- that his own plates had been switched for "trick plates" by the photographer. This seems to have been the standard operating procedure for many of the so-called "spirit photographers" of the day, as was described in the *Scientific American* article referenced earlier in this chapter. Many spirit photographers , including a Mr. Parkes, who produced a number of psychic images, even allowed themselves to be observed while working on the plates. Parkes, for instance, had an aperture cut into the wall of his darkroom so that investigators could see inside while he went through the developing process. The problem was that the investigators had no idea just what plates he was actually developing.

In 1874, a French photographer named E. Buguet opened up a studio and also began a career capturing the spirits on film. Most of his photographs were of famous people, most of who claimed to recognize the extras as deceased loved ones and family members. This did not stop him from being arrested for fraud and tried by the French government though. He admitted deception but even then, there were many who refused to accept his confession as genuine, claiming

This questionable spirit photograph was taken by E. Buguet in 1874. The photographer was later arrested and charged with fraud.

that he had been paid off by the church to plead guilty. In his confession, he stated that his photographs were created by double exposure. He would dress up his assistants to play the part of a ghost, or would dress up a doll in sheet. This figure, along with a stock of heads, was seized by the police when they raided his studio. Buguet was fined and sentenced to a year in prison. Even after this, his supporters continued to insist his photographs were real. Reverend Stainton Moses, the famous medium, was convinced that at least some of Buguet's spirit photographs were authentic. He said that the prosecution of the case was tainted by religious officials, that the judge was biased or that Buguet must have been bribed or terrorized to confess.

The 1870's saw the first general acceptance that there might be something credible to at least some aspects of spirit photography. A number of references to it appeared in issues of the *British Journal of Photography* and in other periodicals of the time. In the 1890's, J. Traille Taylor, the editor of the Journal, reviewed the history of spirit photography and detailed the methods by which fraudulent photos were sometimes produced. He approached the phenomenon as a true skeptic, not immediately disbelieving it, but studying it in a scientific manner. He used a stereoscopic camera and noted that the psychically produced images did not appear to be in three dimensions. He used his own camera and he and his assistants did all of the developing and photographing. Strangely, they were still able to produce mysterious results.

In 1891, the practice of spirit photography gained more credibility when Alfred Russell Wallace, the co-developer of the theory of evolution, spoke out with the belief that spirit photography should be studied scientifically. He later wrote about his own investigations into it and included a statement that he believed the possibility of it was real. He felt that just because some of the photos that had been documented were obviously fraudulent, that not all of them could be dismissed as hoaxes.

Despite such notable interest in the field, little was heard of spirit photography (outside of Spiritualist circles) for a number of years. In 1911, spirit photography entered the mainstream with the publication of the book *Photographing the Invisible* by James Coates. It covered dozens of cases of spirit photographs in detail and was later revised and expanded in 1921. It remains one of the most comprehensive books on the subject during this period and it managed to bring spirit photography into the mainstream for the first time.

Following the publication of the book, several noteworthy articles appeared on spirit photography, including one by James Hyslop, a Columbia University professor. He wrote an introduction to a series of experiments carried out by Charles Cook of two American spirit photographers, Edward Wyllie of Los Angeles and Alex Martin of Denver. Cook did extensive work with the two men in 1916 and provided them with his own plates and had them developed by a commercial studio. In this way, he eliminated any opportunity that the two men might have had to doctor the images. Cook concluded that the photographs submitted were genuine but in these cases thought the name "psychic photography" better matched the phenomenon. He believed that the two men actually produced the images through some psychical means, rather than actually photographing ghosts.

In addition to the photos created by Wyllie and Martin, there were a number of spirit photographs that appeared in those days for which critics could find no plausible explanation. We will review some of these photos in the pages ahead. Despite the failure to debunk many of these photographs, the reality of them was not accepted by the scientists of the day. As it is today, the majority of them simply refused to examine the data and assumed that fraud was more than adequate to explain the findings. One of the few exceptions was Sir William Crookes, the distinguished chemist and physicist. For 30 years, he was a member of the Royal Society and was known for his discovery of thallium, his studies of photography and other scientific work. At the invitation of several skeptical members of the Royal Society, he agreed to take on a six month study of psychic phenomenon. Instead of just six months though, his work continued for years and he came to the conclusion that much of what he studied (including psychic photographs) was genuine. He presented his findings in both book and article form but soon became discouraged about convincing most of his scientific colleagues of the reality of what he was doing. He endured ridicule and disdain, but never wavered from his beliefs. More than 25 years later, he would maintain that spirit photography could, and did, exist.

As time passed and photographic techniques and equipment became more advanced, researchers began to discover that some of the photographs being taken in allegedly haunted locations could not be explained away as film flaws and tricks of light. Gone were the days of phony photos that were taken by so-called spirit mediums in studios. They had been replaced by often accidental photos that defied all logic.

One of the most convincing photographs was the famous image of the "Brown Lady" of Raynham Hall in Norfolk, England. The photo was taken by Captain Provand, a professional photographer, who was taking snapshots of the house for Britain's *Country Life* magazine in September 1936. His assistant,

Indre Shira, actually saw the apparition coming down the staircase and directed Provand to take the photo, even though the other man saw nothing at the time. The resulting image (shown in the coming pages) has been examined by experts many times, although no explanation for it has ever been given. And this was just one of many.....

So, what are we to make of the reality of spirit photographs?

The emergence of modern science in the first half of the 1800's had helped to dispel the superstitions of the past but scientists were unable to connect the mysterious evidence obtained by spirit photography to the progress they were making in other fields. Because of this, most of the investigation and research into the field was carried out by Spiritualists, who believed that far too many of the photographs were genuine, thus validating their often unpopular beliefs. The debunkers of today simply point to the usually ridiculous images that were produced as proof that the entire field was corrupt. However, this is the sort of short-sighted thinking that has managed to stall the study of the paranormal and to prevent it from becoming an accepted field of science.

Today, researchers in this "pseudo-scientific" field have come to realize that the ability to photograph the unseen is no more improbable than the discovery of latent images was back in the early 1800's. Attitudes toward aspects of the supernatural continue to undergo radical changes and move slowly toward acceptance, even though these types of photos still involve an infringement on scientific assumptions and rules. In spite of this, evidence of a common ground between psychic phenomena and physics continues to grow and the times grows ever closer when perhaps the two will come together and explain just how spirit photographs are produced.

SOME OF HISTORY'S MOST FAMOUS SPIRIT PHOTOGRAPHS

There have been those among us who have been attempting to take photographs of ghosts since the days when cameras were little more than newly invented curiosities. What could be better proof of their existence than the ability to capture a spirit's image on film? Unfortunately, many "spirited" efforts have led to failure and, even worse, outright fraud.

Trickery was introduced in the early days of the photographic process, which coincided with the heyday of the Spiritualist movement. In those days, scores of photographers began capturing photos that included faint images that were alleged to be their customer's deceased loved ones. Business boomed until someone noticed that the "Spirit Faces" resembled a number of people who were still alive. The "spirits" in the photographs were soon recognized as double exposures and over-printed images and many of these new mediums were arrested on charges of fraud.

Despite our familiarity with trick photography and our knowledge of the clever hoaxes carried out by the spirit photographers of yesterday, phony spirit photographs still manage to flourish today. Why? Because in addition to fraud, we are often forced to deal with literally thousands of photos that allege to be ghosts that are merely mistakes caused in processing or during the actual photography. Camera straps, reflections and light refractions are often mistaken for ghosts on film and it has become generally accepted to ghost researchers that if you see a photograph for which doubt exists, it is better to discard it than worry too much about it. If it may not be a ghost --- it probably isn't one.

But that's certainly not to say that no authentic photos of ghosts exist!

In fact, there have been a number of such photos that have been taken over the years for which no clear explanations exist. Photos have sometimes appeared for which no evidence of fraud, trickery or mistakes can be discovered. The photos presented in the pages that follow were all deemed legitimate by a variety of sources over the years. In each case, the photographer claimed to be surprised by the end results of the photograph and

This Series of Photos, from a Spiritualist séance at Camp Chesterfield, Indiana, once stunned researchers. Although largely dismissed the photos have remained controversial and debate continues both for an against their authenticity.

experts have looked over the photos and yet have found no explanations for the images that were captured on film. However, the authenticity of each remains for the reader to decide.

Perhaps the most famous ghost photo of all time is that of the "Brown Lady of Raynham Hall". In September 1936, photographers Captain Provand and Indre Shira, were commissioned by Lady Townshend of Raynham Hall in Norfolk, England to take a series of photographs of the house for *Country Life* magazine.

This was certainly not the first appearance by the "Brown Lady", as she was called, and according to some accounts, she had been appearing for centuries. Raynham Hall dates back to the 17th century, and has been in the hands of the Townsend family from that time. The Brown Lady is believed to be the ghost of Lady Dorothy Townshend, wife of Charles Townshend, 2nd Viscount of Raynham. Dorothy was the sister of Sir Robert Walpole, Charles' one-time partner with whom he had a falling-out. It was also rumored that Dorothy, before her marriage to Charles, had been the mistress of Lord Wharton, "whose character was so infamous, and his lady's complaisant subserviency so notorious, that no young woman could be four and twenty hours under their roof with safety to her reputation". Charles suspected Dorothy of infidelity. And, although according to legal records she died and was buried in 1726, it was suspected that the funeral was a hoax and that Charles had locked his wife away in a remote corner of the house until her death many years later.

Dorothy's ghost is said to haunt the oak staircase and other areas of Raynham Hall. In the early 1800s, King George IV, while staying at Raynham, saw the figure of a woman in a brown dress standing beside his bed, noting that her face was pale and hair disheveled. After this though, Lucia C. Stone recorded the first reference to the ghost in 1835, when the ghost made an appearance on

Christmas night. Lord Charles Townshend had invited a number of guests to the hall for the Christmas festivities. Among them was a man called Colonel Loftus, who witnessed a figure in a brown dress with another guest named Hawkins. He described her as an aristocratic looking lady but with a face that glowed with an unearthly light and empty sockets where her eyes should have been.

The next sighting was by Captain Frederick Marryat, an adventurer and an author of sea novels, although no firm date is given for this encounter. In most accounts, the captain asked to stay in the haunted room because he believed that the haunting was the result of local smugglers. He was returning to his room with two companions, when they saw a figure with a lantern coming towards them. They ducked into a doorway, and the figure turned and grinned at them in a "diabolical manner". Marryat, who was armed, fired off a shot, which passed straight through the figure and lodged in the opposite wall. Moments later, the apparition vanished.

The next publicized sighting occurred in 1926, when Lady Townshend stated that her son and his friend had witnessed the ghost on the stairs. They identified the figure as being the woman in the portrait hanging in the haunted room.

The famous photo of the Brown Lady was taken ten years later in 1936. Shira and Provand were just setting up their equipment for shots of the grand staircase when Shira saw what he described as " a vapoury form which gradually assumed the shape of a woman in a veil", he said.

"Captain Provand took one photograph while I flashed the light," he later wrote. "He was focusing for another exposure; I was standing by his side just behind the camera with the flashlight pistol in my hand, looking directly up the staircase. All at once I detected an ethereal veiled form coming slowly down the stairs. Rather excitedly, I called out sharply: 'Quick, quick, there's something.' I pressed the trigger of the flashlight pistol. After the flash and on closing the shutter, Captain Provand removed the focusing cloth from his head and turning to me said: 'What's all the excitement about?'"

Provand was amused by his friend's excitement, maintaining (even afterward) that he had seen nothing on the stairs. In fact, he admitted that he thought Shira was delusional. However changed his mind after the plate was developed when he saw the phantom outline of a human figure on the stairs. Thanks to Shira's insistence, there were three witnesses to the development of the negative. Shira wanted an independent observer to verify the event so he contacted a chemist named Benjamin Jones, who managed the premises above where the development studio was located, and asked him to come down. He observed the entire process and later testified that nothing had been tampered with. A full account of the experience was published in *Country Life* magazine on December 26, 1936.

The photo was later examined by experts at the *Country Life* offices, where it was declared unlikely to have been doctored. There have been a few detractors saying that Shira hoaxed the image by smearing grease on the lens or moving in front of the camera, but there is still no definitive explanation for the photo. It is still held in the offices of *Country Life* today. Experts who have since examined it were puzzled and agreed that the image was not the result of any form of trickery.

Author and researcher Thurston Hopkins also studied the photo and he too declared it genuine. "It may well be the most genuine ghost photograph we possess," he added, "and no study of the supernatural is complete without a reference to it."

The photo shown here is the famous "Lord Combermere Photograph", which was first published in 1895. It gained almost instant fame among psychic researchers and remains a mystery to this day. The photo was part of an account by Miss Sybell Corbett who took the photograph in December 1891 while staying with her sister at Combermere Abbey in Cheshire, England.

Lord Combermere was a British cavalry commander in the middle 1800s, who distinguished himself in several military campaigns. Combermere Abbey was founded by Benedictine monks in 1133. In 1540, King Henry VII kicked out the Benedictines, and the Abbey later became the Seat of Sir George Cotton, Vice Chamberlain to the household of Prince Edward, son of Henry VIII. In 1814, Sir Stapleton Cotton, a descendent of Sir George, took the title "Lord Combermere" and in 1817 became the Governor of Barbados.

The photo that appears here was actually taken in the splendid library of

the house and the camera was placed with a long exposure of about one hour, details of which were carefully noted in Miss Corbett's photographic diary.

Although no one was in the room at the time of the exposure, the developed plate showed the head, body and arms of an older man, seated in a high-backed chair to the left side of the room. The photo was shown to a relative of Lord Combermere and she announced that it did resemble the man. The strangest thing about the photo was that, at the time it was taken, Lord Combermere was attending a funeral at the local churchyard in Wrenbury, a few miles away. The funeral was his own! Lord Combermere had been killed a few days earlier in a road accident in London when he was struck by a carriage.

The photo caused quite a stir and attracted the attention of Sir William Barrett, an investigator for the Society of Psychical Research. He experimented with a similar photo process and then first dismissed this photograph as an unintentional mistake. He surmised that a servant had entered the room while the shutter of the camera was open, sat down in the chair and then left, leaving behind a faint, and rather "ghostly" image.

After further investigation though, Barrett reconsidered. He later learned that the image did not resemble any of the servants in the house and that all of the male servants had been away attending their master's funeral anyway. He confessed to being perplexed and the photograph remains mysterious today.

The next photo was taken in 1959 by Mrs. Mabel Chinnery in a British churchyard. She had just finished photographing her mother's grave and then took a picture of her husband, who was waiting for her in the car. He was alone in the auto at that time, yet the developed photograph clearly showed Mrs.

Chimney's mother in the back seat of the car. A photo expert examined it for a British newspaper and declared the photo to be authentic. In fact, he went as far as to declare, "I stake my reputation on the fact that this picture is genuine," he said.

Perhaps the most famous spirit photograph ever taken by William Mumler, the man credited for first introducing spirit photography to the world, was that of Mary Todd Lincoln and what appears to be the apparition of her late husband, President Abraham Lincoln.

According to Mumler, a small woman who was heavily veiled and wearing a black dress came to his New York studio one afternoon. Giving her name as Mrs, Tydall, she admitted that she did not have an appointment but requested that she be photographed. Mumler later wrote: "I requested her to be seated, went into my darkroom and coated a plate. When I came out I found her seated with the veil still over her face. I asked if she intended having her picture taken with her veil. She replied 'When you are ready, I will remove it!'. I said I was ready, upon which she removed the veil and the picture was taken." It was only when Mumler saw the print that he realized that his mysterious customer had been Mary Lincoln.

"The picture of Mr. Lincoln is an excellent one. He is seen standing behind her, with his hands resting on her shoulders, looking down with a pleasant smile," Mumler said.

The photograph, whether genuine or not (and most believe it is not) simply offered Mary more proof that the spirit world was among us. She had been a believer in Spiritualism since the death of her son Willie, which occurred while the Lincoln's were in the White House. Mary hosted and attended numerous séances and after her husband was assassinated, began delving even deeper into the movement. Before her death, her son Robert had her institutionalized for a time because he feared for her mental health.

This photo is another that has become quite famous over the years. It shows a hooded figure that seems to float on the steps of the altar at England's Newby Church. The photo was taken in the 1960's by the Reverend K.F. Lord, who was merely photographing the front of the sanctuary. He reported that he saw no such figure at the time the photograph was taken. He stated: "The shrouded image appeared only after the photograph was developed."

Two chemists that Lord hired to run tests on the photo could not agree on an explanation but many members of the congregation simply came to believe it was a ghost, relating that the church had been haunted as long as they could remember.

The next photograph is another fascinating one. It depicts a cowled figure that was photographed by a Canadian tourist, Reverend R.W. Hardy, a retired

clergyman from British Columbia, in 1966. He intended simply to photograph the elegant spiral staircase (known as the "Tulip Staircase") in the Queen's House section of the National Maritime Museum in Greenwich, England. Upon development, however, the photo revealed a shrouded figure climbing the stairs, seeming to hold the railing with both hands. Experts, including some from Kodak, who examined the original negative concluded that it had not been tampered with. It's been said that unexplained figures have been seen on occasion in the vicinity of the staircase, and unexplained footsteps have also been heard.

The photo has been examined many times over the years, but thus far, it has withstood all allegations of fraud. Some believe it may be a "ghostly mistake" however. It has been suggested that if a person had hurried up the stairs during a long exposure photograph, the blurring of this person may have created the illusion of a hooded monk. The "hood" could have been nothing more than the ascending person's shoulder. This seems possible but only if a number of variables are taken into account --- like the fact that Reverend Hardy was using something other than a snapshot type camera and that he did not notice, while standing just a few feet away, that someone ran through the frame and ruined the shot. These suggestions, while certainly plausible, seem unlikely.

The following photo was taken by Gordon Carroll of Northhampton, England in 1964. The church was called St. Mary the Virgin in Northhampton and it was deserted at the time the kneeling monk was captured on film. It was not seen to the naked eye.

Another mysterious photo was actually taken by the famed magician Harry Houdini. During the 1920's, Houdini was well known for his debunking of fraudulent Spiritualist mediums and for his natural explanations for much of the alleged evidence that purported to be paranormal. On at least one occasion though, Houdini found that he didn't have all of the answers.

His handwritten record about this photograph was contained in his files, dated in Los Angeles on April 11, 1923. He was approached in reference to photographs that were to be taken of Mrs. Mary Fairfield McVickers who, before she died, requested that photographs be taken of her body at 5:00 on the afternoon of her funeral. According to reports, she claimed that she would appear in spirit form at that time. Mrs. McVickers made this unusual pronouncement on the occasion of her 73rd birthday in July 1922. She told her friends at the First Spiritualist Temple of Los Angeles, where she was a member, that she had experienced a vision of her approaching death.

Mrs. McVickers died the following April and a friend of the woman, Albert H. Hetzel, contacted Houdini and told him about the request the woman had made for a photograph to be taken of her body. Houdini was intrigued and so he got in touch with a friend and movie producer named Larry Semon about borrowing a camera man.

On the afternoon of the funeral, Nathan B. Moss, who worked for Keystone

Press Illustration Service in Hollywood arrived with his camera and plate holders loaded with 14 negatives. Houdini had not told the man what they would be photographing and he and Moss went to a place called Howland and Dewey, Kodak representatives in Los Angeles. When they arrived at the camera store,

they asked for a dozen 5 x 7 plates and the clerk, Frank Hale, pulled out four packages of 12 each. Mat Korn, a customer in the store and a stranger to Houdini, was standing nearby and he was asked to choose one of the packets. Houdini purchased the package of plates and he and Moss entered the darkroom on the premises and removed the plates that Moss had already placed in the camera. He replaced them with the brand new plates, then placed all of the loaded plates into his camera. A few moments later, they left for the church so that they could arrive just before 5:00.

At the church, the body of Mrs. McVickers had been placed in a white, open casket, surrounded by flowers, located at the right of the pulpit. Moss then took 10 photographs of the scene and each of them was taken under the same time exposure of three minutes.

After the photos were taken, the men left and went immediately to the Keystone Press Illustration office. The plates were immediately developed in Houdini's presence and, on one of the plates, they noticed a peculiar streak. Houdini wrote that "Mr. Moss made a print from this plate which caused a great deal of talk. Not one photographer could explain how this could be tricked. Mr.

Moss offered a hundred dollars to anyone who could produce it under the same conditions, whereas no one could duplicate it."

The photograph with the mysterious light was the second one taken. The streak was a heavy band of light that started a few inches from the floor and then extended up to about two feet above a five foot high black screen that had been placed between the open casket and the auditorium At the upper end of the streak, the light became a diffused, glowing mass of a larger shape than the trail that descended from it.

A number of photographic experts studied the plate but stated that because of the nature of the image, it would have been practically impossible for it to have been caused by a defective plate, plate holder or camera.

This mysterious photograph is connected to an even greater mystery that occurred some years ago aboard the oil tanker the *S.S. Watertown*.

In December 1924, a tragic accident occurred aboard the tanker. Two seamen, James Courtney and Michael Meehan, were cleaning a cargo tank while the ship was on its way to the Panama Canal from the Pacific coast. Both men were overcome by fumes in the hold and died from asphyxiation. In maritime fashion, they were both buried at sea on December 4, 1924.

The following day, the "phantom faces" of the two men first appeared. That same afternoon, the ship's captain, Keith Tracy, received a report from his first mate that two faces were following the ship in the water. Because Meehan and Courtney were popular and had many friends on board, Captain Tracy first assumed the sighting was borne out of grief and depression over the men's deaths. Soon, however, he was also at the rail with the rest of the crew, staring at what appeared to be two men in the water, who were keeping pace with the ship. They were within 40 feet of the figures when Monroe Atkins, the ship's chief engineer cried, "It's Courtney and Meehan!". The tanker slowed near the two men but they vanished.

All of the crew, including Tracy, agreed that the apparitions were of the two dead men and they witnessed the faces appearing daily as the ship made its way from the Panama Canal to New Orleans. As the ship changed direction, so did the figures, and they kept pace with the vessel as the voyage progressed.

When the ship docked, the Captain reported the bizarre events to officials at the Cities Service Company, who were naturally skeptical. However, J.S. Patton, a supervisor, suggested that Tracy try and photograph the faces on their next voyage. Tracy's first mate owned a camera and volunteered to try and obtain proof of the strange apparitions. Apparently impressed with the testimony of the men on board the ship, Patton gave a sealed roll of film to the captain, who then officiated as the camera was loaded.

Almost as soon as the *Watertown* left the docks, the phantom faces reappeared. Six photographs were taken of them but the film was re-sealed and not developed until the ship returned to New Orleans. It was then delivered personally to J.S. Patton, who sent it to a commercial developer. Five of the photographs showed nothing, but the sixth revealed the clear images of two ghostly faces. Those who knew the men in life quickly identified them as Courtney and Meehan, the two seamen who had lost their lives in the ship's cargo tank.

Ten years later, a highly inaccurate account of the story behind the faces appeared in the Cities Service Company's own magazine, Service. It attracted the attention of a paranormal investigator named Hereward Carrington and he began delving into the facts of the case. He attempted to interview those who were involved first hand in the incident, but both Patton and the first mate of the *Watertown* had died. The ship's captain and most of the original crew had since dispersed or retired and could not be located. Carrington was able to interview the manager of the company's New York office though, a man named Storey. He was able to confirm that the office had once displayed a blow-up of the snapshot that had featured the ghostly faces in it. The photographer who had developed the film could not be traced and even more disappointing was the fact that no official report had ever been placed on file in New Orleans.

Carrington was able to glean other facts from the manager though. He learned that the strange figures only appeared on occasion, coming and going and lasting only for a few seconds each time. Strangely, they also seemed to appear in the exact same location around the ship each time. They were also always the same size, a little larger than life-size, and always stayed the same distance from one another. Unfortunately though, he was never able to get a look at the original photograph.

In 1957, another investigator, Michael Mann, also became intrigued by the story. He spent more than five years tracing the facts behind the case and was eventually able to secure a copy of the photo. He also learned that after the photos were taken and sworn to by Captain Tracy and his assistant engineer,

Monroe Atkins, the film was checked for fakery by the Burns Detective Agency. The negatives were returned to Tracy and became the property of the owners of the ship.

As the case was never solved or debunked, authors like D. Scott Rogo maintained an interest in it over the decades. He posed a number of interesting questions --- if the figures were so clear that the entire crew saw them, then why did only one of the six photographs testify to their existence? He guessed that perhaps the faces were "real" enough to be collectively seen, but not always clear to be photographed. However, he also realized that whatever force created the images was not strong enough to support their appearance for more than a few moments at a time.

Ultimately, the case remains an unsolved mystery of the supernatural. The phantom seamen eventually faded away and were never seen again. Their disappearance marked the end of one of the greatest and most baffling stories of the sea.

Sir Arthur Conan Doyle will always be best remembered as the creator of the cynical, deductive reasoning Sherlock Holmes but in his later years, he became a proponent of Spiritualism. His conversion lost him many friends, earned him much criticism and some cruel quarters even spread the word that Conan Doyle had gone senile. The Cottingley Fairies affair seemed to be proof of this.

Conan Doyle as the subject of one of the hundreds of alleged spirit photos that he collected over the years

Thanks to his fascination with Spiritualism and the supernatural, Conan Doyle collected a huge number of spirit photographs, most of which he believed to be genuine. In 1922, he penned a book on the subject called *The Case for Spirit Photography*. Unfortunately, the vast majority of the photos that Conan Doyle championed appear blatantly fake today, the obvious result of fraud and double exposure. He became particularly involved with the group of spirit photographers led by William Hope of Crewe. The so-called "Crewe Circle" produced several hundred alleged spirit photographs during its heyday and Doyle posed for a number of them. Not surprisingly, all of the developed plates portrayed spirit "extras" lurking over his shoulder. The credulous author believed all of them to be authentic.

Doyle's fascination with unusual photographs led to what most would offer as his greatest embarrassment in the early 1920's. He was never embarrassed by the photographs or the outcome however, although not for the reasons that most might think. He simply could not conceive of the idea that the whole thing could have been a hoax!

Elsie Wright and Frances Griffiths in a photo taken at the "magical beck"

In 1920, Conan Doyle received a letter from a Spiritualist friend, Felicia Scatcherd, who informed him of some photographs that proved the existence of fairies in Yorkshire. Conan Doyle asked his friend Edward Gardner to go down and investigate and Gardner soon found himself in the possession of several photos which showed very small female figures with transparent wings. The photographers had been two young girls, Elsie Wright and her cousin, Frances Griffiths. They claimed they had seen the fairies on an earlier occasion and had gone back with a camera and photographed them. They had been taken in July and September 1917, near the Yorkshire village of Cottingley. Doyle's acceptance of the photographs, and his writings about them, would galvanize the Spiritualist community -- and would provide the greatest ammunition for his critics.

The two cousins claimed to have seen the fairies around the "beck" (a local term for "stream") on an almost daily basis. At the time, they claimed to have no intention of seeking fame or notoriety. Elsie had borrowed her father's camera on a host Saturday in July 1917 to take pictures of Frances and the beck fairies. According to their account, Mr. Wright developed the photos late that day, revealing anomalous white shapes that gradually moved toward the foreground of the photographs. They looked like sandwich papers or some sort of birds to Wright, but Elsie insisted they were fairies. Mr. Wright took no notice of it but then, one month later, Frances photographed Elsie with what the girls claimed was a gnome. Arthur Wright questioned the girls about it but they stuck to their story -- they simply took photos of what they saw there. They were banned from borrowing the camera from that point on.

Wright was amused by the photos and to appease his wife (who was a believer), he combed

Photograph of Frances (taken by Elsie) with the fairies in July 1917

the area around the beck and searched for signs of either fairies or fraud. He found neither and since the photos had a novelty value, he made a few prints of them to show the neighbors. However, Wright's wife, Polly, was a member of the Theosophical Society (founded by Madame Helena Blavatsky), which flourished in an atmosphere of belief and excitement about the impossible. It was at a local meeting of the society - which, incidentally, was a lecture on fairies of all things -- that Polly confided to her friends about her daughter, her niece and the photographs of the fairies.

Doyle's friend, Edward L. Gardner, was a Theosophist himself and had no trouble believing that the photographs were authentic. Even though the photographs were extremely questionable (and the fairies later turned out to be cutouts from *Princess Mary's Gift Book*, 1915), Gardner pronounced them genuine and obtained copies for Conan Doyle, who was wary of them at first. He began seeking other opinions, including from Sir Oliver Lodge, who immediately pronounced them as fakes. Doyle had other ideas about the photos though. He was not sure that they were actually fairies but they were certainly mysterious figures. Obviously, the girls were central to the issue -- could they be gifted mediums? He sent Gardner back up north to meet with them and to investigate the "magical" beck. Doyle meanwhile left for Australia on a lecture tour and left Gardner to cope with the media storm that surrounded the revealing of the photographs. The newspapers, not surprisingly, were not open to the possibilities of fairies and the City News even stated that "It seems at this point that we must believe either in the almost incredible mystery of the fairy -- or in the almost incredible wonders of faked photographs".

Unknown to the newspapers and to Gardner and Doyle, the girls had taken three more fairy photographs during the summer of 1920. One of them showed an obviously two-dimensional fairy with fashionably bobbed hair offering a flower to Elsie and another depicted a "fairy bower" in a tree (an ectoplasm-like cocoon) that was very exciting to Conan Doyle. The third was of a leaping fairy that the girls claimed was captured on film during its fifth leap.

(Left) A "fairy" offers flowers to Elsie

(Above) Photo of Elsie and the gnome, September 1917

Conan Doyle was intrigued but still bothered by the photographs and so he asked for an opinion about them from the Eastman Company and from Kodak, although he never waited for their answers before declaring them the real thing. He published an article about the fairies in the Christmas 1920 issue of the *Strand Magazine* and soon was deluged with photographs from others who also claimed to have seen their own fairies. Conan Doyle examined them all, but saw none which appeared to be as genuine as the Cottingley photographs. He later penned a book in 1922 called *The Coming of the Fairies*, which detailed the entire account of the affair.

To look at these photographs today, the modern eye can easily see them to be fakes. In defense of Conan Doyle however, we have to realize that first and foremost, he was a gentleman and he believed that because he treated others with kindness and honesty, they would treat him in the same manner. Needless to say, he was taken advantage of on many occasions. On this occasion however, it would have never crossed his mind that the two girls might be lying about the photographs. Even if he had doubted them, he would have never accused them of dishonesty, for it was just not his way.

In the early 1980's, the two women finally admitted the photographs were a hoax. They stated that they had faked them to get back at adults who teased them for saying they played with fairies. The joke had just gotten out of hand when Gardner and Doyle got involved and by that time, it was too late to back out. They promised to each other that they would reveal the truth once all of the principles in the case had passed away, especially Conan Doyle, who they did not want to embarrass when it came out the photos were not real.

Strangely though, even though they eventually admitted the photos were not real -- they did maintain that they had really seen fairies in the beck. The photographs were staged to show their parents just what they had seen. In fact, despite their confessions, Frances went to her grave maintaining that one of the famous photographs was actually real. Which one? We will never know for sure...

3. GHOSTS ON FILM: HOW DOES IT WORK?

The main problem in regard to the production of spirit photography is that no one knows how these genuine images find their way onto plates and film. Equally important is the fact that no one knows what these spirit images are themselves.

Fred Gettings

There is no doubt that the camera has become one of the most important tools used by the ghost hunter to collect evidence of ghosts and strange phenomena. Since the days when investigators were debunking mediums and ghost hunters like Harry Price were prowling Borley Rectory, the camera has been an essential part of paranormal investigations. In the pages ahead, we will examine the various types of phenomena which is sometimes captured on film, from the ever popular images referred to as "orbs" to the documentation of actual physical phenomena that occurs in a haunting.

In years past, photographers who called themselves "mediums" were largely responsible for the field of spirit photography. The field in those days was riddled with fraud, which damaged the reputation of ghost research in ways that continue today. But far removed from its namesake during the Victorian era, spirit photography today involves many kinds of advanced techniques. Despite the gains in technology, it is still (and should be) subjected to the same kind of scrutiny now as it was then. It is imperative that a good ghost researcher knows all that he can about his camera and how it works because one of the most important parts of your investigation will be the photographs that are taken and later examined for evidence of the paranormal. For this reason, it is vital that your entire team is well aware of your "protocols" for using cameras in your investigations. Spirit photography involves many kinds of advanced (and several basic) techniques that can be used to try and capture ghosts and "spirit energy" on film. One of the purposes of this book is to provide some information for best using your camera during investigations and also some methods and ways to be sure that what you are getting on film is actually something paranormal.

To start with, it shouldn't matter what sort of technology you are using to try and obtain spirit photos if the photos themselves cannot stand up to the scrutiny of a practiced eye. In other words, just because someone claims that they have a photo of a ghost, does not necessarily mean that they do. Often, anyone with any experience with photography at all can spot the claims of those who want to "believe" they have a ghost photo. There are many problems that can occur, even with the most simple cameras, from double exposures, tricks of light, camera straps, lens refractions and even obvious hoaxes.

But how does taking photographs of ghosts actually work? How do ghosts end up on film when they cannot be seen with the human eye?

Unfortunately, no one really knows just how ghosts end up on film. Some believe that it has something to do with the camera's ability to freeze a moment of time and space in a way that the human eye cannot do. This may also combine with the intense energy pattern of the ghost, which somehow imprints itself through emulsion onto the film itself. This is the reason why many researchers recommend that the ghost hunter does not load his film into his camera until he actually reaches the place that he plans to investigate.

In addition to those theories, it has also been suggested that ghosts, or paranormal energy, may be at a different spectrum of light than we are used to. This light spectrum may be one that is not visible to the human eye and yet the camera manages to sometimes pick it up.

This spectrum of light may have a lot to do with radiation that is caused by electromagnetic energy, which many researchers feel that ghosts may be made up of. The range of electromagnetic radiation extends from the short range energy expended by electrical appliances to the longest radio waves. Although we can only see the spectrum of visible light, photographic emulsions are more sensitive and, for this reason, we can actually photograph further than we can see beyond the visible spectrum, including some portions of electromagnetic energy. This is one possible explanation for the extra images that appear in spirit photographs.

Electromagnetic radiation travels like waves of water. The wavelength (that is the distance from one wave crest to the next) determines the color of the visible light and the intensity of the light related to the height of the waves. Very short waves are called x-rays when they are produced by the x-ray tube and gamma rays when they are given off by an atomic reaction. They are measured in terms of nanometers and one nanometer is equal to about one-millionth of a millimeter. Our eyes can only see waves that are between 400 nm (violet) and 700 nm (deep red) but bees can see ultra-violet light and snakes can detect their prey by its infrared emissions. All photographic emissions are sensitive to blue and ultra-violet light but can also be made sensitive to all wave lengths from x-rays through ultra-violet and visible light and on into the infrared range, which has waves a little longer than the deepest red light that we can see with the naked eye.

X-ray photographs are shadow photographs that are taken on special photographic emissions made for this purpose. However, ordinary photographic emulsions are also sensitive down to very short wavelengths. The high cost and danger involved in using the special equipment necessary prevents most of us from conducting paranormal experiments using x-rays at haunted locations but by adapting our own cameras, we can also do successful work with ordinary and infrared film.

Photography is about making pictures with light. Light passing through the lens of a camera forms an image on light sensitive film. This image, which is invisible, is called a latent image and is made into a permanent visible image when the film is developed. In black and white, negative-positive photography, this development involves several steps, each of which is simple but necessary. The latent image is formed by exposing the film in a camera, the film is developed to bring out the image, rinsed to stop any further development, fixed by converting any unused sensitive chemicals into a soluble state, washed to remove the soluble residue and then dried. This provides us with a negative that must be printed by a similar process, usually onto a sheet of light-sensitive paper, to give us a positive picture. Colored prints are made by a more complicated but basically similar process.

Most photographs are only produced when light from the subject is collected and directed by the camera lens in a way that re-creates an image of the subject on light-sensitive film. Paranormal photographs are taken in the same way that standard photographs are but many of them show extra images that were not visible when the photographs were taken. Is this a case of the camera and film picking up a different spectrum of light?

Most photographic emulsions depend on the silver halides for their sensitivity to light. These halides are salts formed by a combination of silver with bromide, chlorine or iodine, a group of elements called halogens. The silver halides in photo emulsions are sensitive to anything from the shortest x-rays to the deepest red light that we can see. However, glass camera lenses absorb radiation that is shorter than about 330 nm, which may explain why the camera can "see" what we cannot. Do paranormal images exist at a shorter or higher wavelength than we can normally see? Perhaps and perhaps this is why the special lenses and filters that have been created for ultra-violet and infrared photography regularly pick up these mysterious extras.

These special filters can actually aid our experiments in spirit photography. Ultra-violet absorbing filters pass visible light but cut out ultra-violet radiation and can help to determine which part of the spectrum in which the paranormal images are present. If they are within the ultra-violet range, the extra images can be enhanced by using a ultra-violet transmitting filter over the lens during investigations. This is a very dark glass filter that cuts out all visible radiation and only transmits the ultra-violet, keeping any visible images from affecting the film. Photographs taken in this manner will show only the paranormal images on the film. For this reason, should you decide to experiment with this, you should use the filter on a secondary camera so that you will still have a record of the location on film.

Invisible infrared rays are found just beyond the other end of the visible spectrum from ultra-violet rays. Anyone with a 35mm camera and the necessary filters can take infrared photographs, although this type of film is both expensive and problematic. Later in the book, we will examine the best ways to use infrared film and some of the problems that can arise with it, because many researchers feel that, in spite of the many difficulties, working with infrared film is well worth the considerable effort.

So, do paranormal images appear just beyond the spectrum of light that we cannot see? This seems to be perhaps the most valid theory as to how ghosts manage to appear on film but as with the idea that ghosts move so fast that we cannot see them or that they "emulse" themselves onto our film - it is merely a theory. How ghosts manage to end up on film may be a combination of any of these theories and for all we know, every one of them is correct -- or perhaps none of them are. As with anything else to do with the paranormal, few researchers are ever in complete agreement as to how something works. Most ghost hunters simply find a method for producing ghost photographs and then adapt it to work in their own research. Most often though, ghosts are captured quite by accident, leaving no clues as to why a particular photo was successful.

Each photo that is taken and is displayed should be under intense scrutiny by the researcher before he presents it to the public. There are hundreds of terrible photos out there that claim to be authentic. Most of them are not and this sort of shoddy ghost research is damaging to every paranormal investigator who is trying to provide legitimate evidence that ghosts exist.

In order to be sure that your own photos are genuine, it's important for you to have a good working knowledge of cameras, films and natural lens effects. I encourage anyone to go out and purchase standard books on photography. You should know your camera, your shutter speeds and what can happen with lens refractions, light reflections and arcs. By doing this, you have protected yourself from the arguments of the debunkers and perhaps have spared yourself some embarrassment by finding your own flaws in some of your photos. Once you understand the natural effects that can occur, you will be confident about the photos you are taking.

I also recommend that you try experimenting with what fake photos look like. Try bouncing your camera flash off of a reflective surface and see if you can make "orbs" appear. Try taking photos in the rain and in poor weather conditions. Also, drop various things like flour, dust and water in front of your lens and try photographing your camera strap to simulate many of the photos that are out there. I think that you will be amazed to find that you have debunked a number of photos that you may have previously thought were genuine.

But what kind of photos can you expect to get when using your camera during an investigation? I have made some references here to paranormal energy and "orbs", but what are they and are they really evidence of ghosts?

THE TROUBLE WITH "ORBS"

There are a number of different types of photographic anomalies that turn up on film during investigations. Many researchers believe that these types of activity portray actual ghosts, but I cautiously refer to it as "paranormal images", or "energy", on film, simply because there are so many unknown variables when it comes to paranormal photography. Some of the strange images on photos that turn up include eerie rays of light, floating objects, mists and shapes and even apparitions that appear to be human, but perhaps the most common images are the so-called "orbs".

Many of the "orb photographs" that turn up on Internet websites or in books seem to come from cemeteries but they actually have an annoying habit of showing up almost anywhere. They have become the most commonly reported types of "paranormal photos" claimed by ghost hunters today. Despite what you might see and hear though, there is absolutely no hard evidence whatsoever to suggest that "orbs" are in any way related to ghosts. Yes, they do often turn up in photos that are taken at haunted locations, but, as you'll soon see, many of these photos have been called into question. However, I do think that legitimate photos of image anomalies (or orbs, if you prefer) exist. These photos do show a type of paranormal phenomena, but just what type that is remains to be seen.

As mentioned, "orb" photos are the most commonly seen "ghost photos" today and you will probably see more photos on the Internet of these purportedly "mysterious" balls of light than of anything else. While I do believe that genuine photographs of paranormal "orbs" exist, they are not as common as many people think. An "orb photograph" is usually one that is taken in an allegedly haunted place and somewhere within the photo is a hovering, round ball. Some of these "orbs" appear to be giving off light, while others appear to be transparent.

Despite the claims, the majority of "orb photos" are not paranormal at all, but merely refractions of light on the camera lens. This occurs when the camera flash bounces back from something reflective in the range of the camera. When this happens, it creates a perfectly round ball of light that appears to be within the parameters of the photo but is actually just an image on the lens itself. Many people often mistake these "orbs" for genuine evidence of ghosts. These false "orbs" can also be created by bright lights in an area where the photo is being taken, by angles of light and by many types of artificial lighting.

When looking at "orb" photos, you will note that most of them occur when the camera flash is used. Some of the photographers will insist that their flash was not on, which means it was and they didn't know it. The automatic exposure control on most any standard 35 mm camera uses fill flash in all but the brightest light. It should also be noted that "orbs" were actually quite rare before digital cameras became common. In the early days of low-cost, cheap digital cameras, some "ghost hunters" actually proposed that digital cameras are "superior for orb photography". And since they were producing more "orb" photos, this was technically true. But the digital imaging chip is very different than traditional film photography and was far inferior until recent times. Some of the earlier, low-end digital cameras were made with CMOS chips and they would create "noise" in low-light photographs that would be mistaken for "orbs". It seemed that when they were used in darkness, or near darkness, the resulting images were plagued with spots that appeared white, or light colored, and where the digital pixels had not all filled in. In this manner, the cameras were creating "orbs", and they had no paranormal source at all.

If all of these problems exist with image anomalies --- "orbs" --- then is there any reason to believe that they might be paranormal at all? I believe that there are legitimate photos of what are anomalous, round balls of light that can be photographed and can sometimes be seen with the naked eye. But how do we tell a real "orb" photo from a false one?

There are a number of determining factors, not the least of which is corresponding activity. By this I mean, photographing an "orb" just after recording a sharp temperature drop, or some other event that can be documented. In every aspect of paranormal research, corresponding activity, and documentation of the activity, is vital to the success of the investigation and to authenticating the activity, evidence and especially the photographs.

The investigator should also look at the photograph itself. In doing so, watch for image anomalies that are especially bright or are especially dense (in other words, you can't see through them). This is important in determining which anomalies are likely genuine because false "orbs" are readily identified by the fact that they are almost always very pale white or blue in color and are transparent. Also, watch for anomalies that appear to be in motion. This can be a very good sign that the image is genuine. I have seen a number of photos that are believed to be genuine in which the anomaly actually moved several feet during the time when the shutter of the camera was open. In situations like this, it's hard to believe that the anomalous object could be anything other than paranormal in origin.

As mentioned though, one of the things that I have noticed about "orb photos" is that the majority of them seem to be taken in cemeteries. I have often been openly critical of ghost hunting in cemeteries. By that I mean, actually just going out to cemeteries and shooting photographs and hoping to capture something on film. While this is great for the hobbyist, I don't feel that it's serious research. Needless to say, I have been harshly criticized for this view. In spite of this, I have not changed my mind about the fact that random "ghost hunting" is not an investigation. And if this isn't reason enough to discourage this kind of activity, I now have another reason for taking this view.

One of the problems that I have had with this type of "ghost hunting" involves the photos that often come back from it. Ghost hunters, with no idea of any corresponding evidence, often come back from cemeteries with copious numbers of "orbs" in their photos. Again, I do feel that some of these anomalies constitute paranormal energy, but most don't, so I decided to try something out on my own.

With three other researchers, I went out to a cemetery that we picked at random on a warm summer night and took several rolls of film. We had no readings, stories or reports to justify the decision, but just took photos anyway. After having them developed, we discovered a number of the photos were filled with semi-transparent "orbs".

On a hunch, we then went to a nearby football field that was roughly the same size as the cemetery we had already visited. We walked around for a few minutes and again shot a few rolls of film. I was unfortunately not surprised to find that these photos were also filled with orbs. Was the football field haunted? Of course not!

What we did was walk around both areas and stir up dust and pollen from the grass. When we took the photos, these particles in the air caught the reflection of the camera flash and appeared to be "orbs". We also discovered that such photos could be taken after walking or driving on a dusty road. The dust particles would reflect the light, just as moisture can do, and make it seem as though the air was filled was "orbs".

I can't help but feel that this might explain some of the photos taken in cemeteries that have been thought to be paranormal in origin. Does it explain them all? No, it doesn't, but such tests and experiments beg all of us to be careful in our research. As I have always maintained, there exist no experts on ghosts or paranormal photography. My thoughts are that if we can discover the ways to rule out the false photos, we have a much better chance to discover which ones might be genuine.

But what about the photos that do seem to be genuine? Over the years, I have collected a number of them from my own research, and for my collection, that seem to show authentic "orbs". The first photograph here was taken in 1997 during the investigation of an Illinois home that had once been a church. The renovated building became the subject of investigations by the American Ghost Society after the owner began to report the sounds of voices in the building at night, as well as apparitions that were wandering around the place. This photo-

graph was taken by investigator John Barrett, who was using a short exposure to take pictures in the living room (former sanctuary) of the home. On the far right side of the photo, a careful examination of the print will show what appears to be an "orb" of some sort in motion. It seems to have traveled several feet --- leaving a trail behind it --- in just the short amount of time that the shutter of the camera was open. Whatever this object was, it had to have been moving at an incredible speed.

The above photograph was taken in a barn located in northwestern Indiana. The snapshot was taken by the owner of the property, an attorney, and is an area of her farm that is reputed to be the most haunted. I have detailed the history of this location in my book *Confessions of a Ghost Hunter* but the site has been the subject of many investigations by the American Ghost Society, the Indiana Ghost Trackers and other paranormal research groups. The owner began reporting strange happenings here shortly after moving to the farm and guests and visitors have had their own strange encounters. Incidents included eerie voices, lights turning on and off by themselves, things vanishing and then turning up again in other places, strange moving cold spots in the house and the barn, water faucets turning on without assistance, odd knocking sounds, a rocking chair that moves by itself and much more. The owner also told me that the farm seemed to have a strange effect on her horses and dogs as well, as they often seemed to see or sense something that wasn't visible to her.

I wrote about my own strange experiences at the farm in the previously mentioned book and can assure the reader that this is a truly haunted place. There have been dozens of paranormal photographs that have been captured here and this photograph is a great example of what may be an authentic "orb" in motion. Like so many other photos, the object was not seen at the time that it was taken and the image simply turned up on the developed film.

This third photograph was taken in 1997 during the investigation of poltergeist phenomena in an Illinois home. This picture requires some explanation. The case from which this photograph comes was connected to a young woman that I have since referred to as "Christine M.". The home where she and her mother lived became the first, and possibly most active, human agent poltergeist case that I ever got involved with. I was initially contacted because Christine believed her house was haunted. She told me of a wide variety of weird phenomena that was taking place like knocking sounds, lights turning on and off, doors slamming, cabinets opening and closing, windows breaking and other destructive happenings. Because she was under 18 at the time, I contacted her

mother about the location and she assured me that the events described were actually taking place. She also agreed that an investigation might be in order.

During this initial interview, I asked her about the history of the location and if she had any thoughts on why the phenomenon was occurring. I also asked how long it had been going on. Her answer surprised me. She explained the phenomena had started just two years before, when Christine had gotten pregnant at age 15. She was very upset at the time and became depressed and anxious enough that her mother had taken her to see a therapist. She stopped going however and the weird activity began a short time later. While Christine believed that the house was haunted, her mother thought that her daughter was somehow causing these things to happen.

With the home owner's permission, I began a series of five in-depth investigations of the house. My interviews with Christine and her family collected numerous accounts of the activity that was taking place. The events began one night when Christine was laying on the living room floor watching television. This was the largest room on the first floor and when I visited the house, it contained a couch, some chairs, a table and a large piano. There were three doors leading into the room, which led to a spare room, a screened porch and to the kitchen. As she and her mother were watching television, the piano began to loudly play by itself. Not long after that, things began to escalate. Soon, doors began to open and close by themselves, windows broke inside of empty rooms and the sounds of knocking and footsteps began to be heard, usually on the upper floor of the house when no one was present. Lights turned on and off, radios turned on and off and the volume of the television would often raise and lower without assistance. The footsteps and noises from upstairs became so bad that Christine insisted that her mother put a padlock on the door leading upstairs. She remained convinced, even after my initial visit and after her mother's insistence otherwise, that the house was haunted by ghosts.

Not surprisingly, the events in the house did not convince her otherwise either. The strangest event that reportedly occurred (and I did not witness this for myself) was when Christine's sister ended up with a horrible bite mark on the back side of her upper arm. There were no pets in the house and no way that the girl could have managed to bite herself in such an area of her body. I don't think that it was any coincidence that the bite mark appeared just shortly after Christine and her sister had an argument.

As you can imagine, I was having some reservations about the house being infested by spirits at this point, especially since her mother again told me that she was convinced that the activity centered around Christine. However, the young woman insisted that the house was haunted and would only agree to the investigations that I had planned if we would proceed as if the house were actually haunted. I reluctantly agreed and the five investigations began. Most of the time, things were fairly quiet, including the two uneventful investigations that were conducted with Christine removed from the house. Not a single trace of any sort of activity was detected when she was not present. However, on two occasions, I was present when violent phenomena occurred.

On one evening, Christine, her mother, three other investigators and myself clearly heard what seemed to be someone banging loudly on the walls of the second floor of the house. There was no one else present at the time but the sounds really seemed to be made by a person upstairs, walking down the hallway and hitting the walls with his fists. Christine's mother told me that these were exactly the sorts of sounds that they had become used to over the past number of months. Unsure of what else to do, I ran up the stairs to see if anyone else was there. The downstairs door, as mentioned, had been padlocked, so Mrs. M. had to open it for me and I hurried up the staircase with another one of the investigators in tow. The pounding noises had stopped by the time we reached the upper floor, but if anyone had been there, we would have found them. Instead, we discovered the hallway and the rooms to be dark, quiet and empty.

During another investigation, on a separate night, I saw two cabinet doors actually slam shut under their own power. The incident occurred while I was in the living room with Christine, her mother and one other investigator. As we were sitting and talking, we began to hear a repeated rapping sound coming from the kitchen. It began to increase in volume until it started to sound like someone rapidly hammering on a wooden surface. The first sound was joined by a second and then a third. Each of the sounds was identical and my first thought was that it sounded just like someone slamming a cabinet door closed. Just as I had done when we heard mysterious sounds upstairs, I ran for the kitchen as quickly as possible. The two rooms were separated by an open doorway, a little wider than usual, and curved into an arch. Hurrying from the carpeted floor and onto the linoleum floor of the kitchen, I slipped just as I was going under the archway. I stumbled but didn't fall and was able to look up quickly enough to see two of the cabinet doors waving back and forth and cracking against the wooden frame. The movement ceased almost immediately as I came into the room but it was certainly the first time that I had ever seen "paranormal movement" during an investigation.

Over the next several weeks, the activity in the house continued but it did begin to decrease after two months. Thanks to the relentless and intrusive interviews that I conducted with Christine and the fact that we conducted the two completely uneventful investigations with the girl removed from the house, I felt that we could determine that the cause of the haunting was indeed Christine. Eventually, her mother and I were able to get her to agree with these findings and she returned to the therapist. Not surprisingly, the phenomena ceased completely soon after and, to this date, nothing else has occurred at her home. She is now happily married and no longer bothered by any strange activity.

In addition to the phenomena that I witnessed, I was also present when one of the other investigators snapped this photograph of a bright ball of light in the downstairs hallway. According to his account, the light was actually coming down the hallway, literally following Christine's little boy, who was two years-old at the time. I was in the kitchen with Christine when this occurred but I did see the resulting photograph, which shows a glowing light (apparently in motion), just a foot or two behind the boy as he is running into the living room. This was a rare occasion when a paranormal object was actually seen at the time that it was photographed.

MYSTERIOUS MIST-LIKE ACTIVITY

In the course of many paranormal investigations, photos have been taken in which strange mists, fogs and streaks appear. These images have no natural origin and were usually not visible to the human eye when the photos were taken. Whether or not these pictures actually show ghosts or not has yet to be firmly determined but they are strange and many of them remain unexplained. I prefer to think of these photos as showing a kind of "paranormal energy", meaning that it is most likely paranormal in origin, although no explanation exists for it yet. These types of photos can be some of the most exciting for a ghost hunter to capture, because, unlike with most "orb" photos, these images are much harder to explain away.

But the researcher still has to be very careful. He should note that when looking at many of the photos on display, the "strange" fogs seem to be very close to the faces of the ghost hunters in the photos. If the weather conditions of that particular investigation are checked, it's likely that it was cold that night. If this is the case, then the images could be vapor from the researcher's breath or some other moisture exuded from the ghost hunter's bodies or equipment. It's also possible that it might be fogging on the lens of the camera. This is usually noticeable by the way that everything in the photo is blurred or distorted.

Over the years, I have also received dozens of photos of this type that are nothing more than cigarette smoke that has been photographed with a flash so that it seems to give off an eerie glow. Thankfully, these don't normally come from investigators (who know better than to smoke during an investigation!) but from the public who discover weird photos on their roll of film and after viewing similar ones on a website, come to believe their photos have ghosts in them. Cigarette smoke is usually distinguishable by the fact that it is very thick and seems to give off a bluish color. An examination of the photo will often even show someone in the frame who is holding a cigarette, which is, needless to say, a tell tale sign that it's smoke in the photograph. The reviewer can also examine the surroundings in which the photograph was taken. If it is a snapshot from a bar or tavern, there is a good chance that it's smoke and not a ghost, whether the place is haunted or not. Unfortunately, whether you can see someone in the photo smoking or not, the location tends to negate the idea that it might be something paranormal in the photo. As mentioned earlier, it's better to err on the side of caution when it comes to the paranormal.

When it comes to searching for a genuine photo of a paranormal "mist" or "fog", the best thing that you can do is to try and take one of your own. In this way, you can be sure of the conditions under which the photos were taken, making sure that no natural fog is present and that temperatures were well above normal at the time of the investigation. You will know that you were not smoking or fogging up your camera lens. You can never be sure of what was going on when it comes to photos from other people.

Another thing to beware of is the tendency that people often have to look for faces, shapes and forms in photos of this type. Don't be fooled into doing this! The human imagination wants to find an explanation for what it cannot explain and in this way, we often create additional phenomena from what was already believable evidence. The energy that has been captured in the photo is already evidence of the paranormal. By trying to pick out shapes and images from the photo (without some sort of other corresponding evidence) we begin to stray towards the mindset of those who are willing to believe anything and will look, not for true evidence, but for anything that might validate our own beliefs.

The tendency to try and create viable shapes from a shapeless mass is called "simulacra" and it normally refers to seeing images in objects like clouds, trees, walls, windows and more. Many sightings and visions of the Blessed Mother can be attributed to "simulacra", especially when it comes to seeing Mary in a tortilla, in water marks and in salt stains on freeway underpasses. There are dozens of incidents that occur each year when people come to believe that such stains and marks are visitations from the Virgin Mary. Are they? It seems unlikely but one thing is sure --- they are a validation of the beliefs of many people and while they may be considered wonderful, one has to question whether or not they are actual evidence of the Blessed Mother's presence here on earth. The same has to be said of similar "paranormal" images that appear in photographs. If no other explanation can be found for such images, they should

 be allowed to stand as mysterious on their o w n . Trying to make them into something they are not does nothing but destroy the credibility that the photo - graphs

already possess.

As mentioned, photographs of mysterious shapes and mists can be some of the strangest that a paranormal investigator might obtain. This first photograph (seen on the previous page) was taken in June 2003 when I was in Philadelphia, Pennsylvania, spending the night at the Eastern State Penitentiary for a television show about ghost hunting. A crew from The Learning Channel had brought myself and several other investigators to the now closed penitentiary for a night of ghost hunting. The photograph was taken in the Death Row section of the prison. I was exploring the entire building and taking numerous photographs that night and snapped this one in the empty corridor. There was no one present at the time and I saw nothing out of the ordinary when the photo was taken.

This second photograph was taken at the haunted farm in northwest Indiana that was mentioned earlier in this chapter. This photo was taken by Michelle Bonadurer during one of the investigations that were carried  out at the location. Strangely, the image that was photographed looked exactly like the anomaly that was witnessed by myself and investigator Rob Johnson in the barn.

While standing in total darkness in the barn, we saw an area near the door that suddenly began to light up with a brilliant, white light. The light seemed to draw itself through the wall of the foyer and into the first horse stall. As it did so, the foyer drew dark and the light caused the back wall of the first stall to be illuminated. The white was bright enough that it cast a glow toward us and through the bars of the stall. It entered the first stall and then with the speed of a fast walk, it passed through the wall of each stall, all the way down the length of the barn and then vanished out the back wall. I later saw the photograph that is reproduced here (although it was taken earlier) and realized that this was almost exactly what Rob and I had seen that night.

One of the most disturbing photographs that I have in my collection was given to me in 1995. This photo is not disturbing because of the picture itself but because of the story behind it. The photo was given to me in person a number of years ago on the condition that I did nothing with it until two years had gone by. Even now, I have declined to release the names of the individ-

uals in the photo or even where the photo was taken. What I will tell you is that the owners of the photo (shown here) were ordinary people, with no interest in ghosts, but who have experienced more than their share of tragedy --- some of which is connected to this photo.

The simple facts are these: The young woman in the right was graduating high school on the night this photo was taken. The man in the photo is her father and the baby is her daughter, born just a few months before. After this photo was developed, the family noticed the strange images that appeared in it, especially around the baby. They really didn't know what to think of them, only that they were strange enough to make them want to

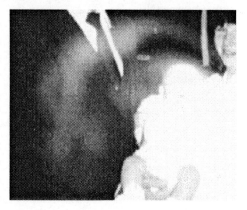

keep the photo around. It was not until the baby died just two months after the photo was taken that the images came back to haunt them. They hung onto the picture for a short time but then after the gentleman pictured here came to see me speak on the paranormal one night, he gave me the photograph.

What is it that appears around the baby in this photo? Is it some sort of paranormal energy? And if so, did it have anything to do with the child's impending death? And further, if the image is something paranormal, was it there to help the child --- or to harm her?

APPARITIONS ON FILM

This is, without a doubt, the smallest section of paranormal photographs that exist. This is due to the fact that such photos are rare and hard to find and that it is usually very hard to prove whether or not the photos are hoaxes or double exposures. I have already presented a number of the most famous "apparitions on film" photographs in this book and later on, there will also be a display of some modern and little known photos of this type.

I wish there were more of these photographs to present to the reader, but regretfully, most that you see of actual apparitions seem to be "too good to be true" and they often are. However, we cannot be too quick to judge in some cases. I have been given hard copies and negatives of a well-known photograph that depicts a ghostly woman. This photo has been criticized in print and in the media but what most readers and viewers don't know is that the critics and debunkers did not have all of the facts. What they do not know (or will not admit) is that the photo that is often seen is only a cropped portion of the entire photo. When the entire print is examined, the researcher can see that the woman in question casts no shadow. Also, I have given this photo (and a negative) to three different professional photographers for analysis. None of these men believed in ghosts and were anxious to tell me that the photo was a hoax. However, they could not and to this day, none of them have an explanation for the image. I will present it for the reader to examine in a later chapter in this book.

In addition to this photo, there are a number of other possibly genuine ones as well. In most cases, researchers have come to believe that the full-bodied apparitions depicted in these photos are probably the result of Residual hauntings. These images can be very much like photographs themselves, repeating their actions over and over again in a constant film loop. Because the energy seems to imprint on the atmosphere of the location, it might be possible for the camera to pick this up. Unfortunately though, as with the other types of photos, no one is sure at this time as to exactly how this can work.

In an earlier chapter, we examined some of the most famous spirit photos in history. For examples of "apparitions on film", I would direct the reader to this earlier section and to the last chapter of the book.

4. GHOSTS ON FILM: CAPTURING THE EVIDENCE

It would appear that on occasion ghosts or something inexplicable can be caught on film. The obvious advice when visiting a haunted house or locality is always carry a camera and always take a few photographs --- especially if you think you see a ghost!
Peter Underwood

The idea of using a camera to investigate the supernatural has been around for more than a century and a half but the paranormal itself has been with us since the beginning of time. The Bible is filled with incidents of the supernatural. Auras, prophetic voices and levitations have been well recorded and attributed to saintly people like St. Francis of Assisi, St. Theresa, St. Joseph of Copertino and others. While these stories may have been written under the influence of emotion and fallible human memory, there is undoubtedly some truth to the accounts. One of the most believable is the story of St. Joseph of Copertino, who was beatified in 1753. It was recorded that his levitation was witnessed by not only the general public but members of his order and on one occasion, by Pope Urban VIII himself. Just imagine if there was a photographic record of this event - and others like it --- and how it might affect our lives and religion today.

Today, we have a great advantage over those of our ancestors who witnessed paranormal events and it is that, since the era of photography, we have been able to make a record of this type of event.

The scientific investigation of psychic phenomena began with scientists in the 1860's who gathered to discuss whether or not Spiritualist mediums could be studied scientifically. The investigations that followed confirmed some of the reports of incidents that occurred during séances and led to Sir William Crookes becoming involved in the speculations as to the cause or causes of these manifestations. The eventual result of this was the formation of the Society for

Psychical Research, which still exists today. There were a number of mediums investigated over the course of the next several decades and many scientists reported and photographed their psychokinetic abilities. Over time, the ability of these mediums to produce levitation and movements without physical contact was established but no real explanation of their talents was ever revealed.

Crookes' investigations led to his experiments with two of the best known mediums of the time, Florence Cook and Daniel Douglas Home.

Daniel Douglas Home

Daniel Douglas Home was believed to have been one of the most powerful mediums of his day. Home was born in Edinburgh, Scotland in March 1833 and his psychic talents, said to have been inherited from his mother, began to show themselves when he was only an infant. His aunt reported that his cradle would rock by itself, as though moved by an unseen hand, and at age 4, Home accurately foretold the death of a cousin. He was a sickly and strange child and believed by his family to have remarkable powers. He was nine when he moved to America and came to live with an aunt in Connecticut. His health continued to decline and he was diagnosed with tuberculosis. Unable to exert himself as most boys could, he spent most of his time walking in the woods and reading his Bible. He came to believe that the spirits of the dead constantly surrounded him.

Shortly after he turned 15, the Fox sisters created a sensation with their table-rapping and Spiritualism was embraced by the public. Not long after, Home's own paranormal talents began to increase. He was living with his aunt, Mary Cook, at the time and she grew to believe that the eerie events that took place around the boy were the work of the devil and she threw him out. For most of the rest of his life, Home had no place of his own to live. Staying in various households as a guest, he traveled about, holding séances for those who were interested. His séances however, were different than most others as he always held them in brightly lit, rather than darkened, rooms. Home had attended many other séances in the past and regarded most mediums as frauds. He decided to do the opposite of what was being done elsewhere, showing the public that he had nothing to hide.

During these sessions, he produced spectral lights, rappings, ghostly hands which ended at the wrist and which reportedly shook hands with audience members, moved tables, chairs and other objects, played spectral music, spelled out messages from the dead using lettered cards and amazingly seemed to be able to shrink his body in size. While he was doing these things, he would ask the sitters to hold his hands and feet to prove that he was not somehow manipulating the objects with secret devices or wires. He claimed that all of his feats were made possible by friendly spirits over whom he had no control.

In August 1852, Home moved beyond what many would consider to be parlor tricks (although darn clever parlor tricks!) and first accomplished the feat that would make him famous. To put it bluntly, Home managed to fly.

The séance where this event allegedly took place was at the Connecticut home of Ward Cheney, a wealthy businessman. Also present that night was a local journalist, F.L. Burr, whose assignment it was to find something incriminating against Spiritualism in general and especially about Home, who had debunkers in an uproar with his excellent reputation. However, instead of writing an expose of the evening, Burr instead wrote:

"Suddenly, without any expectation of the part of the company, Home was taken up into the air. I had hold of his hand at the time and I felt his feet - they were lifted a foot from the floor. He palpitated from head to foot with the contending emotions of joy and fear which choked his utterances. Again and again, he was taken from the floor, and the third time he was taken to the ceiling of the apartment, with which his hands and feet came into gentle contact."

But how was this accomplished? Home claimed not to know himself. He stated that an "unseen power" simply came over him and lifted him into the air. Needless to say, most readers who came upon this article (and it was re-printed many times) were skeptical, as are most who come across it today. Full-body levitation is, and always has been, considered impossible. Throughout history, only a few saints had ever been alleged to be able to lift themselves from the ground in such a manner, although today, some practitioners of strict meditation techniques claim to be able to manage a few inches from the floor. Who knows? But in the middle 1800's, there was only one man, Daniel Douglas Home, who could levitate without the aid of mirrors, ropes or even a safety net.

In 1855, Home traveled to Europe, where he began associating with the rich and famous. He conducted séances in England and on the Continent, gaining supporters and wealthy patrons. In 1858, he was married to the daughter of a Russian nobleman with whom he had a son, Gregoire. His wife passed away in 1862.

In 1866, the Spiritual Anthenaeum was founded with Home as the Secretary and soon after, he became embroiled in a scandal involving a wealthy widow who would later claim that Home tried to bilk her out of a large sum of money. Home maintained that the money was freely given for his "spiritualistic services" and the widow did not demand the return of the fortune until he refused her sexual advances. The trial became an embarrassing affair and many of Home's supporters abandoned him. When it was over, he was forced to return the money.

During the scandal, Home was apparently at his best when it came to producing incredible phenomena. In December 1868, his most famous feat took place at the home of Lord Adare. During the evening, Home reportedly went into a trance and floated out the window of the third floor, then floated back in another window --- all before the eyes of a number of stunned witnesses. The event occurred in front of three irreproachable members of London's high society ---- Lord Adare, his cousin Captain Charles Wynne and the Master of Lindsay.

(Left) A dramatic illustration of one of Home's reported levitations. Did he accomplish the impossible? (Right) The Brazilian medium Carmine Mirabelli was allegedly photographed here as he hovered near the ceiling without the assistance of ropes, pulleys or strings. A trick photograph?

Skeptics contend the event was a mass hallucination or was somehow accomplished through trickery. They base this on the fact that there are slight discrepancies in the accounts of Adare and Lindsay, mostly concerning the size of the windows that Home floated out of, how high they were off the ground and whether or not the night outside was dark or moonlit. The debunkers ignore the statement of Captain Wynne, which was simple and straightforward. "The fact of Mr. Home having gone out of one window and in at another I can swear to," he wrote. "Anyone who knows me would not for a moment say I was a victim of a hallucination or any other humbug of the kind."

It should again be noted that during Home's entire spectacular career, he was never seriously accused of fraud (all of those accusations have come much later) and he was never caught cheating, as so many of the mediums of the day were. It is also worth noting that this feat, like his other levitation, was accomplished in the home of someone that he was visiting for the first time and was among people of limited acquaintance. Any opportunity that he had to rig up elaborate machinery or engage the services of an accomplice to do so was nonexistent. There is no evidence to say that he ever resorted to such tricks.

In 1871, Home married again and that same year began a series of tests with Sir William Crookes, a scientist interested in Spiritualism. To determine if Home could somehow manipulate electro-magnetic energy, Crookes wrapped an accordion in copper wire and then placed it in a metal cage. He ran an electrical current through the wire, which he believed would block any magnetic energy coming from Home. The medium was still able to make the accordion play, leading Crookes to believe that he possessed an independent psychic force.

Over the course of 50 séances, Home managed to produce psychokinetic phenomena in front of at least 30 people. Sounds appeared to come from pieces of furniture, the floor and from walls and were often accompanied by vibrations that were perceptible to touch but had no natural or mechanical cause. Movement of heavy objects also occurred and during one experiment, a heavy table lifted from the floor numerous times. Crookes also wrote that: "My own chair twisted around, my feet not touching the floor. Under the eyes of all present a chair moved slowly from a distant corner of the room. In another case, an armchair came up nearly to where we were sitting and at my request moved back about three feet. On five different occasions, a heavy dining room table rose from a few inches to a foot and a half off the floor while I held the hand and feet of the medium."

Crookes also wrote: "One of the most amazing things that I have seen was the levitation of a glass water bottle and tumbler. The room was well lit by two strong alcohol-soda flames and Home's hands were far distant. The two objects remained suspended above the table, and by tapping each other, answered 'yes' to questions. They remained suspended above the table for about five minutes, moving in front of each person and answering questions. We verified that Home was entirely passive during the whole time and that no wires or cords were employed. Home had not entered the room before the séance."

Russell Wallace, who was also present for many of the séances, stated that Home was an outstanding and indisputable example of psychokinesis.

In 1873, after two years of testing with Crookes, Home announced that he was retiring. Tired and in poor health, he traveled with his wife and son until his death from tuberculosis in 1886.

After his death, dozens of explanations were given about how Home accomplished his feats through trickery, but not a single one of these theories was ever proven. In addition, the most prominent stage magicians in the world all claimed they could duplicate his stunts on stage, but for some reason, they never did.

Another medium that was investigated by Crookes was Florence Cook. In these investigations, Crookes made liberal use of photographs and managed to record not only Cook's séances but incidents where she allegedly manifested the entire form of her "spirit guide", Katie King. This was really the beginning of cameras being used in paranormal research but the end result is regarded today as being questionable at best.

During the heyday of Spiritualism, Florence Cook became one of the movement's most famous mediums. She was noted for her ability to produce full-form spirit materializations, especially those of her spirit guide. Katie already had a long history before being forever attached to the persona of Florence Cook. She first appeared during the initial Spiritualism craze of the 1850's and graced many séances. Like her spectral father, John King, "Katie" was not her real name. In life, she was said to have been Annie Owen Morgan, the daughter of the pirate Henry Morgan, who had been knighted and appointed governor of Jamaica. He preferred to be known as "John King" in the afterlife though and his daughter adopted his name. In life, Annie Morgan had been a self-professed liar and cheat, as well as a thief and an adulteress -- and all this before she died in her twenties. Her new mis-

sion in death was to prove to the world the truth of Spiritualism and, of course, to prove the talents of a few mediums in particular. One of these was Florence Cook...

Florence (or Florrie, as her mother called her) was born in the east end of London in 1856 and as a child claimed that she could hear the voices of angels. Her mother would later state that she had always been aware of the presence of spirits but her psychic gifts only began to manifest at age 15, when she levitated a piece of furniture during a table tilting session with friends. When she was still an adolescent, she began conducting séances in her home, where she became known for being able to manifest "spirit faces". Florence created a makeshift spirit cabinet by sitting inside of a large cupboard

Florence Cook

in her family's breakfast room. A hole had been cut high up on the door and it was here where the faces would appear.

Florence would climb into the cabinet and would allow herself to be bound to the chair with ropes about her neck, waist and wrists. The door would be closed and the sitters would sing a hymn to create the proper mood. The cabinet door would be opened again to show that Cook was still tied to the chair, then closed again. A few moments later, the faces would appear in the opening. When they finally vanished, the doors would be opened again and Florence would be revealed, still tied to her chair and apparently exhausted from allowing the spirits to use her energy and appear.

A few people noticed that the faces, which were draped with a thin white cloth, looked an awful lot like Florence. They suggested that the girl simply slipped her ropes, stood on the chair to stick her face through the hole, then tied herself back up again. Nevertheless, the audience loved her performances and she soon gained a following. Many were impressed by the fact that she never charged a fee for her séances and others came merely because she was an attractive young lady.

With that in mind, it's no surprise that the pretty young girl quickly became famous. In addition to her looks, her séances had other appeals as well, including the fact that the spirits had a habit of tossing Florrie into the air and, on at least one occasion, ripping her clothing off. While Florence basked in the new found attention, some of her friends, and her employer, were becoming unsettled by her new gifts. Miss Eliza Cliff for one, in whose school Florence worked as an assistant teacher, was reluctantly forced to discontinue her employment. The girls in the school were unsettled by the strange happenings that seemed to occur around Miss Cook and their parents were afraid that the young ladies might become affected themselves. The headmistress was quite fond of Florrie but was "compelled to part with her."

By 1872, full-form materializations had become very popular at séances and one night, in that same year, a white face appeared in the darkness outside the curtains of Florrie's spirit cabinet. The floating mask was announced to be that of "Katie King", who was already a spirit to be reckoned with in America. But Katie was not the mysterious and ethereal figure of Spiritualist writings -- she was a proof of the resurrection of the dead, a spirit made flesh and a young woman who could walk and talk among the sitters. Her new body was almost indistinguishable from that of a living girl --- a beautiful young lady that unfortunately bore a very close resemblance to Florence Cook.

As with most Spiritualist mediums of the day, Florrie preferred to enter her trances within the confines of her spirit cabinet, where her psychic energies would be built up. After as long as 30 minutes might pass, the curtain would part and a figure, dressed all in white and looking quite pale, would emerge as Florrie continued to lie unconscious in the cabinet. Occasionally, while Katie was present, Florrie could be heard sobbing and moaning inside of the cabinet, as if the manifestation was draining the energy from her. During Katie's first appearances, the spirit would simply smile and nod at the audience, but later, she began to walk amongst them, offering her (strangely solid) hand and talking to them. She was fond of touching the sitters and allowing them to carefully touch her as well. After Katie returned to the cabinet, Cook would be found, still tied up and drained of energy.

It was believed that spirit forms, like Katie, were actually made up of a mysterious substance known as ectoplasm, which was emitted from the medium's body and took on unexplained shapes. It was generally regarded during the heyday of the movement that interfering with ectoplasm, or with the body of the entranced medium, could be dangerous to the medium's health. If this is true, then on one occasion, Florence Cook had a very close call...

While it was highly improper for sitters to grab at the spirits, or the medium, during a séance, it did sometimes happen. On the night of December 9, 1873, one of the sitters at a Cook séance was a man named William Volckman. Although an invited guest, he apparently became quite agitated by the "obvious" similarities between the medium and the ghost. In a fit of anger, he jumped up and grabbed Katie by the wrist, announcing loudly that she was Florence in disguise. For a spirit, Katie put up quite a fight and managed to succeed in leaving several bloody scratches on the man's nose! Katie was finally rescued by Edward Elgie Corner, Florence's fiancée, and by the Earl and Countess of Caithness and barrister Henry Dunphy, who were friends of the Cook family and aware of the inherent danger in interfering with an apparition. They seized Volckman and a scuffle ensued, allowing Katie to make her escape. According to Dunphy, she disappeared, dissolving from the feet upward. Volckman was determined to follow up on his assault though and he rushed to the cabinet. Here, he found no sign of Katie but he did find Florrie with her clothing in disarray, but still tied up.

Was this a case of a skeptical investigator gone berserk, or something else? It is significant that shortly after this incident, Volckman married another famous London medium named Mrs. Samuel Guppy, who was very jealous of Florence and her fame. The incident with Volckman did not immediately harm Florrie's career as a medium, but it did shake the faith of some. She suffered a slight reversal of fortune for a time and began looking for a new angle to pursue to garner some much needed good publicity.

At about this same time, medium Daniel Douglas Home was undergoing testing by the eminent scientist Sir William Crookes. Florrie quickly got in touch with Crookes and offered to add her own contribution to psychical research. Crookes was delighted to investigate the now famous partnership of Florrie and Katie King and happily agreed to a series of private séances. Shortly after, what many consider to be the most problematical investigations of the Spiritualist era began...

Almost at the start of the investigations, Crookes invited Florence, and occasionally her mother and sister, to come and stay with him at his home on

Mornington Road in northwest London. Mrs. Crookes was in the house, but was not around much, as she was expecting their tenth child at the time and was usually confined to her room.

The first time that Crookes had experienced Katie had been when Florrie had first approached him about the investigations. He had visited the Cook home and took part in a séance. During the sitting, Katie had appeared from behind the spirit cabinet curtain and had asked Crookes to accompany her behind it. According to his account, he saw Katie standing over the unconscious form of Florence Cook, still bound with sealed tape. According to Crookes' account, he checked three different times to be sure that the woman on the floor, illuminated by a dim gas light, was actually Florence and he was convinced that she and Katie were separate individuals. Was this proof that Katie really was a ghost?

One of the few remaining photos from the Florence Cook seances. This photo shows Crookes walking arm in arm with Katie. during one of the sittings

Perhaps -- but not all of the sitters at her séances were completely convinced. Many of them insisted on extreme measures to prevent Florence from practicing trickery. Customarily, before the séance would begin, Florrie would be bound with a cord or sealed with tape. Each time, the bindings were found to be still intact at the end of the evening. And although the indignities that were later inflicted on mediums (such as filling their mouth with fruit juice to prevent ventriloquism and checking all of their orifices for secreted ectoplasm) were never pressed onto Florrie, her hair was nailed to the floor on at least one occasion. Believe it or not, Katie still appeared but the experiments that followed were not without controversy.

In 1874, Crookes began testing Florence and he produced a number of photographs of Katie King and was allowed to document her appearances with

Florence in plain sight. During the test, Cook laid down on a sofa behind a curtain and wrapped a shawl about her face. Soon, Katie appeared in front of the curtain. Crookes checked to be sure that Cook was still lying on the sofa and he saw that she was -- although incredibly, he never moved the shawl to be sure that it was really her.

Crookes created 55 photographs of Florence and Katie but only a handful of them remain today. The rest were destroyed, along with the negatives, shortly before his death in 1919. Crookes used five cameras, two of them stereoscopic, operating simultaneously during the sessions. Many of the photos were both poorly shot and questionable in authenticity and while many of them purported to show both Katie and Florence at the same time, they mainly played right into the hands of the debunkers.

In one of the remaining photos, we see Crookes walking arm in arm with the spectral Katie but even the most casual observer can see the obvious facial similarities between Katie and Florence. In another, we see Katie standing in the background while Florence is slumped (apparently in a trance) over a chair in the foreground. Unfortunately though, Katie's face is hidden by an "ectoplasmic" shroud. In a third, very strange photograph, we see a blurred Katie staring directly into the camera and an odd sitter on the left who is actually a reflection in a mirror. On the right side, we see one half of a medium who is supposed to be Florrie but could be anyone. Strangest of all though is the fact that Katie is kneeling, or appears to be, on some article of furniture that is covered to look like an extension of her dress. Katie was said to be four inches taller than Florence but if this was to create some

This photo was supposed to prove that Florrie and Katie were two separate beings but unfortunately, Katie's face is completely obscured by an "ectoplasmic" shroud.

extra height, it was badly done. It resulted in making her dress bunch at the knees and her legs appear ridiculously long.

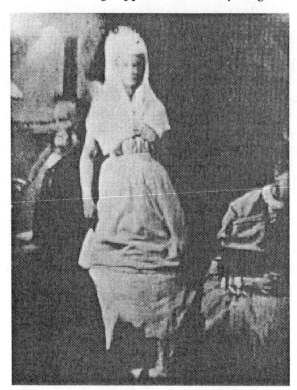

The strangest of the Crookes photos shows a mirror image of a sitter on the left, half of what is apparently Florence on the right and Katie standing atop a piece of covered furniture.

Crookes was called into question about his testing but he rushed to the defense of his subject. He stated that Florence agreed to every test that he submitted without question and that he had never seen the slightest inclination on her part to try and deceive him. "Indeed, I do not believe that she could carry on a deception if she were to try," Crookes wrote, "and if she did she would be certainly found out very quickly, for such a line of action is altogether foreign to her nature."

Crookes may have been convinced of the genuineness of the Cook-King collaboration but his critics were not. Katie looked so much like Florrie simply because that's who she was, the skeptics said. It was not simply good enough to cite Crookes' integrity and his stature as a scientist to convince someone of the authenticity of the séances. Crookes' defenders cited this however and they still do today. They also say that it was impossible that Crookes might have had a sexual relationship with Florrie, which would explain his willingness to help her perpetrate fraud, just because his wife was also present in the house. And while no evidence of such an affair exists, it would be naive of us not to consider the possibility of it.

There are four possible explanation for the seemingly unexplainable events that occurred between Crookes, Florence and Katie:

1. That the scientist became embroiled in an affair with Florence under his wife's nose and that he colluded with her to manufacture fraudulent results for the Katie King investigation.

2. That Crookes was enamored with the girl, or her alter ego of Katie, and that he kept up the pretense that he believed her act to save face and to keep her close to him.

3. That Florence employed a double to pretend to be Katie King. This is not as outrageous as it might sound. During the investigations, a young medium named Mary Showers stayed in the Crookes' residence while Florence was there. She performed a double act with Florrie as the two of them would go into trances together and would create two materializations, one of Katie and one of "Florence Maple", who bore more than a passing resemblance to Mary. Would it not have been possible for Mary or even for Florence's sister to have simply stepped in to pretend to be an unconscious Florrie, slumped over and usually covered, while Florrie walked about as Katie King?

To most modern readers, the accounts of Katie's manifestations contain many clues about the nature of Florence and her possible alter ego. Katie flirted and teased, wandering about the darkened room and sitting on laps, touching and being touched and on one occasion even stepping out of her robes to reveal her naked form. "Now you can see that I am a woman," she said. Could Katie have been a way for the repressed young lady of the Victorian era, as Florrie undoubtedly was, to act out her innermost desires? And if so, was she doing it consciously -- or had she actually convinced herself that the manifestation of Katie was real?

4. And our final explanation -- that Florence was a genuine medium, that Katie was real and that Crookes' investigations were completely genuine. Although Crookes behaved strangely for a man with a scientist's regard for detail, such as omitting names and addresses of witnesses from his record, this may have been in regard for Florrie's strict rules of secrecy.

In addition, we can look to the eyewitness accounts of the séances that survive. According to Mrs. Ross-Church, who was better known as the novelist Florence Marryat, Katie resembled Florrie in some ways but was remarkably different in others. She stated that Katie was taller and heavier than Florence and that Katie had red hair, while Florrie's hair was dark and almost black. Crookes had also noted a number of differences between the two young women. Katie was taller, heavier and broader in the face, had a fairer complexion and longer fingers. Florrie had pierced ears, Katie did not. One one occasion, Florence had a large blister on her neck but when Katie appeared, her neck was as fair and smooth as usual.

Unbelievably though, as when he failed to check under the shawl, Crookes took no comparison photographs to show the pierced and unpierced ears or the length of the girls' fingers. Or if he did, he left no record of them. This seems amazing in that Crookes was investigating a phenomenon that could theoretically change the way the world believed.

In 1875, Katie sadly announced that she would soon be leaving Florence and that her time on earth would soon be at an end. Crookes later wrote of a scene that he witnessed when Florence and Katie said their final goodbyes. According to his account, Katie made one last appearance in the séance room and then walked over to where Florrie was lying on the floor. She touched the medium on the shoulder and implored her to wake up, explaining that she had to leave. They talked for a few moments until "Miss Cook's tears prevented her from speaking". Crookes was asked to come over and hold Florence in his arms, as she was falling to the floor and sobbing hysterically, and when he looked around, the white-robed figure of Katie was gone.

With Katie now gone, there was no point in Florrie staying on for further investigations. In fact, she revealed to Crookes for the first time, that she had married Edward Corner about two months before. Florence went into a sort of retirement for six years but then returned to the Spiritualist scene manifesting a new spirit, this one named Marie. This new spirit partner managed to provide even more entertainment that Katie had, singing and dancing for the sitters at her séances. There was something about "Marie" that was beginning to bother people though...

At a séance in 1880, Sir George Sitwell noticed that Marie's spirit robes covered corset stays, so he reached out and grabbed hold of her. He held on tightly to her and when he pulled aside Florrie's curtain, he found that the medium's chair was empty. He was not surprised to discover that he was holding onto Florence, clad only in her underwear.

After that, Florence would only perform if someone were tied up in the cabinet with her. On at least one occasion, Florence Marryat participated and she later testified that during Marie's appearance, she was firmly tied to Florrie in the cabinet. This wasn't enough to keep her audience though and Florence Cook vanished into relative obscurity as a housewife in Monmouthshire. She gave her last séance in 1899 and passed away in 1904.

William Crookes was stunned by the overwhelming criticism from his fellow scientists over his investigations of Florence Cook and he soon gave up active investigations, although he remained a staunch supporter of psychical research until his death. He was knighted some 20 years after his work with Florence, because during his long and distinguished career he discovered the element thallium and his experiments with vacuums led to the discovery of the cathode ray tube and x-rays. His obvious contributions to the world of paranormal research have only been recognized in recent years by enthusiasts in the field but there is no question that without his groundbreaking experiments, we would not have the information that we have today.

Despite the harsh response that Sir William Crookes received concerning his experiments with Daniel Douglas Home and Florence Cook, investigations into psychic phenomena continued and it was increasingly done using cameras. Shortly after the turn of the last century, many scientists and psychic investigators began to theorize that much of the activity reported during séances, from table turning to moving objects, could be attributed to the psyche of a living person rather than to the discarnate personalities of the dead, as the Spiritualists had claimed. Crookes and many others were already considering this idea two decades before but it was now becoming more of an accepted idea.

Psychokinesis is the ability to control the movement of objects mentally, without touching them or influencing them physically in any way. Spontaneous examples of this ability are referred to as "poltergeist activity" and the name "poltergeist" is a German word that literally means "noisy spirit". This kind of activity includes the inexplicable movement of objects, their unexplained appearance and disappearance and the production of knocking, tapping and noises. It usually occurs in the presence of young adolescents, often young women, who are usually emotionally disturbed. This paranormal energy manages to fling household objects and heavy furniture and can affect electrical lights, telephones and appliances. Both the controlled manifestations of psychokinesis and the poltergeist outbreaks are of such a nature that it makes it possible for researchers to not only thoroughly investigate them but to do so using photographic techniques. Such techniques began to be used more and more and into the 1930's, investigators who were still studying the phenomena created during séances captured fantastic photos of tables, chairs and small objects that were somehow lifted into the air and flung about --- often to the startled expressions of sitters in the circle. Many of these dramatic photos still survive today, providing credible evidence of strange powers at work.

In addition, investigators of poltergeist outbreaks also began to employ cameras in their research and these snapshots also proved to be very exciting for psychical research. There have been dozens of authentic photos that have been published over the years showing poltergeist activity as it occurred. A few of them have been reproduced here. In addition, investigators were also able to document the aftermath of the attacks as well, providing strong evidence that something paranormal was at work in the locations.

Perhaps the most famous "poltergeist photo" of recent years occurred during the Tina Resch case that took place in Columbus, Ohio. The outbreaks in the home were thoroughly investigated and witnessed by scores of people but it was not until the famous photograph of the "flying telephone" was taken that the case blew wide open and gained national attention.

In March 1984, the John and Joan Resch family included their son, Craig, their adopted daughter, Tina, and four foster children. That month, their 14-year old daughter Tina had become the focus for a strange and very frightening series of events.

On a Saturday morning in March 1984, all of the lights in the Resch home suddenly went on all at once, even though no one had touched a switch. John and Joan assumed the incident had been triggered by a power surge and they telephoned the local utility company. It was suggested that they call an electrician, which they did. An electrical contractor named Bruce Claggett came to the house and he assumed, as did John and Joan, that it was simply a problem with the circuit breaker. However, he soon learned differently. He was unable to make the lights stay off and even went as far as taping the switches in the off position. As fast as he could tape them however, the lights would turn back on. Closet lights that operated with a pull string would be turned out, but seconds later, the bulbs would be glowing again. Claggett finally gave up, unable to explain what was going on.

By evening, stranger things were being reported like lamps, brass candlesticks and clocks flying through the air; wine glasses shattering; the shower running on its own; eggs rising out of the carton by themselves and then smashing against the ceiling; knives were flying from drawers; and more. A rattling wall picture was placed behind the couch, only to slide back out again three different times.

As the weekend wore on, a pattern began to develop. The intensity and focus of the activity seemed to be Tina, who was even struck by a number of the objects. A chair was seen tumbling across the floor in Tina's direction and it was only stopped from hitting her because it became wedged in a doorway. Family members, neighbors and unrelated witnesses actually saw Tina being hit and smacked by flying objects, which came from opposite sides of the room from where she was standing.

Near midnight on Saturday, the Columbus police were summoned to the house but there was nothing they could do. The only respite from the strange events came on Sunday, when Tina left the house for church and then again in the afternoon when she went out to visit a friend.

By Monday morning, the house was a wreck and literally dozens of reliable witnesses, including reporters, police officers, church officials and neighbors, had reported unexplained phenomena in the Resch home. Desperate for help, the family turned to the news media for an explanation. When reporters for the *Columbus Dispatch* arrived, they also witnessed the strange happenings but one of the reporters, Mike Harden, knew of Dr. William G. Roll's work on similar cases and suggested to Mrs. Resch that she contact him immediately.

Dr. Roll arrived in Columbus on March 11. As the Project Director of the Psychical Research Foundation in Chapel Hill, North Carolina, he had long been considered the country's leading expert on poltergeist phenomena. Roll was born in Bremen, Germany in 1926, where his father was the American vice-counsel. He graduated from Berkeley in 1949, where he studied philosophy and psychology, the closest fields he could find to psychical research. In 1950, he went to England to study at Oxford and with support of the Society for Psychical Research and Eileen Garrett, he set up a small research laboratory, where he worked from 1952 to 1957.

While at Oxford, Roll got in touch with J.B. Rhine at Duke University in North Carolina. In 1957, he invited Roll to come to Duke and a year later, he was sent, along with fellow parapsychologist J.G. Pratt to investigate a poltergeist at Seaford, Long Island. Their report concluded that the disturbances were most likely the result of unconscious manipulations by a young boy in the family. Roll and Pratt coined the term "recurrent spontaneous psychokinesis" (RSPK) to explain these types of cases. It is in general use today as another name for poltergeist activity.

Since that time, Roll had investigated well over 100 cases of poltergeists, both modern and historical. From his reports and personal observations, Roll determined that there were patterns of RSPK effects in the reportedly "haunted" locations. These inexplicable, spontaneous physical effects repeatedly occurred when a particular person was present. He believed that the activities were expressions of unconscious PK carried out by the individual acting as the agent.

His past research certainly made him qualified to study the events in Columbus but even so, he had little idea of what to expect from the case. He had come at the direct invitation of Joan Resch, after seeing the case widely reported in the newspapers. He ended up spending a week in the house and while the poltergeist activity seemed to calm just after he and his assistant arrived, it made a noisy return by the end of the week.

The most impressive events occurred on March 15, when Roll observed a brief flurry of activity first hand. The incidents that he witnessed took place when he and Tina were alone on the second floor of the house. As things began to happen, Roll stayed very close to her and left his tape recorder running so that he would have an accurate account of the events. A slamming sound came from the bathroom as what Roll believed to be a bar of soap was thrown from a dish on the sink. He and Tina walked into the bathroom and then emerged again. As they did so, a picture on the wall to their left suddenly fell to the floor. Roll had the girl under observation the entire time and saw no movement on her part.

However, Tina did become upset because the picture was one of her mother's favorites. Fortunately, it was not broken, but the nail had been ripped out of the wall. Roll offered to nail it back up again and began to do so when the poltergeist once again began to react.

"I was keeping Tina under close watch throughout this period," Roll later reported. "So when I hammered in the nail, she was standing right next to me and I was very aware of her exact position and what she was doing. Before I proceeded, I placed my tape recorder on the dresser, which was behind us and to our left. As I was hammering in the nail, we heard a sound like something falling to the floor. We turned around and my tape recorder was on the ground." The recorder had somehow managed to travel about nine feet, seemingly without assistance. Roll could see no way that Tina could have touched it.

Roll had been hammering the nail back in with a pair of tongs that he had found on the dresser. When he was finished, he had laid them back down again. During the few moments that his attention was focused on the traveling tape recorder, the tongs had also been flung from the top of the dresser and had landed about six feet away. Tina had been nowhere near them at the time.

Not surprisingly, as the case made national news, cries of fraud and hoax began to be raised by the debunking community. Three representatives of the Committee for the Scientific Investigation of Claims of the Paranormal showed up at the Resch house unannounced on March 13, while Roll was still investigating. One of the group members was the debunker and magician James Randi, who had already publicly attacked the case in the press. The CSICOP investigators became more skeptical when the Resch's refused to allow Randi into the house. They had no objection to the other two investigators, both scientists, but would have nothing to do with Randi. Because of this, the entire team decided to withdraw (for reasons that remain unclear) and began to issue negative statements about the case, even though they had never actually investigated it.

But it would be the sensational photograph that was taken in the house that would galvanize people all over the country.

When John and Joan Resch contacted the news media about the strange events in their home, one of the reporters who responded was Mike Harden, who wrote for the Columbus Dispatch. It would be Harden who would suggest to the Resch family that they contact Dr. William Roll. Harden also got in touch with a professional photographer named Fred Shannon, who had worked for the *Columbus Dispatch* for 30 years. These two veteran newsmen would make national news themselves with their involvement in the case and would release a series of photographs that would shock the world.

Shannon received the first call from Harden on March 5, 1984. He phoned him directly from the Resch home, a pleasant, two-story, stucco house in a nice part of the city. Harden asked him to come to the house immediately and Shannon packed up his gear to leave, never realizing that he was about to embark on one of the most bizarre assignments in his career. Even the words of warning from Harden over the telephone did not prepare him for what he was about to experience. His experiences in the Resch home would be brief, but his later testimony about what he saw would become compelling evidence of the paranormal.

Shannon was met at the door by Mike Harden when he arrived. He was introduced to the Resch's and they began to explain to him about the strange happenings that had been taking place. The "force", as they were calling it, was hurling household objects all about the place and the majority of the disturbances seemed to be aimed at their daughter, Tina. They began to show him about the house, starting in the dining room, where the chandelier had been damaged by flying wine glasses, as well as by other objects that had been hurled from the walls and had crashed into it. The force had almost completely destroyed the long-stemmed glasses that the Resch's kept in the room. When Shannon arrived, only one glass remained on the portable bar in the corner.

After looking over the damage for a few minutes, John and Joan Resch went into the adjoining kitchen, leaving the photographer alone in the dining room with Mike Harden and Tina. Moments later, they followed the girl's parents into the other room and, within seconds, they heard the sound of glass shattering in the dining room. "Uh-oh," Joan Resch groaned, "there goes the last wineglass." They raced back into the dining room and found the splintered remains of the glass in the opposite corner from where it had been.

The now perplexed photographer followed the rest of the group back into the kitchen a few minutes later and to his surprise, found that the force again chose that moment to react again. A tremendous clatter was heard in the dining room and when they returned, they found that six metal coasters (which had also been sitting on the portable bar) had sailed through the air in the same direction as the last wineglass. They now lay in a scattered pile near the broken pieces of glass.

According to Shannon, they soon entered the kitchen uninterrupted and the Resch's told him about all of the things that had happened in the room. For example, "all hell broke loose" whenever Tina opened the door to the refrigerator. Eggs would fly out and burst on the ceiling, jars would overturn, containers of leftovers would burst open and expel their contents onto the floor. On one occasion, a stick of butter had erupted from the icebox and had sailed across the room to become lodged between two cabinet doors. Instead of slowly sliding to the floor though, the butter inexplicably began moving upwards toward the ceiling.

The Resch's then took Shannon into the living room. They explained about the time that a large, overstuffed chair chased Tina out of the room, cartwheeling until it slammed into the wall and dislodged a picture. Shannon was intrigued by the story, so he decided to take a photo of the chair and the picture, the whole frame of which was still intact although the glass was shattered. He asked Tina to pose next to the chair and to hold the picture so that he could see it through the lens.

At that same instant, when he shot the photo and the flash went off, Shannon heard a loud crash. Tina claimed that something knocked the picture out of her hand. Shannon was thinking that she had just dropped the picture and the crash when it hit the floor was what had startled him - but he soon had second thoughts about this. He quickly noticed that she was still holding the corner of the picture in her hands, as if something had struck the picture with force and had knocked it out of her hands, leaving her holding one small corner of it.

Unnerved and upset, Tina sat down on a couch in the family room on the opposite side of the kitchen. As Shannon and Harden turned to go back into the kitchen, they heard a tremendous booming sound! Without thinking, Shannon immediately turned and snapped a photo. The developed image would later show Tina covering her head - the lamp on the stand next to her had crashed to the floor.

Since his eye was not on her at the time, Shannon was unable to say for sure whether or not Tina knocked over the lamp herself, but he was confident that she had not. "I had swung around so rapidly," he later said, "that I don't see how she would have had time to knock over the lamp and so completely cover her head. She was covering her head because she had been attacked by so many various objects. She was a badly frightened girl and her fear never left her all during the time these things were going on. At this point, I had been in the house for 15 minutes!"

Tina sat down on the arm of a chair across the room from the couch where she had been sitting. Shannon took up a position in the doorway near a love seat, with his back to the kitchen. Suddenly, the love seat that was close to him began to move towards Tina. It pivoted on one leg and shuffled toward her about 18 inches! Needless to say, the skeptical photographer was startled --- but not so much so that he was unable to snap a photo of the shocked expression on Tina's face. "I knew the photo wouldn't mean much to someone who wasn't there, as I was, to see what had happened", Shannon explained. "Anybody who chose to think that way would say it was just a setup. So I was looking for other things to happen. I didn't have long to wait."

Shannon and Harden decided to observe the girl more closely and took a seat on the couch, with Tina on the loveseat, facing them. On the floor in front of her was a colorful afghan, which Joan Resch had earlier explained had once rose off the floor and had covered Tina. Within a few moments of the journalists sitting down, they saw this repeated and Shannon took a photo of her with the afghan draped over her body. He had no explanation for how it could have lifted from the floor and could find no method as to how Tina could have accomplished this on her own.

Later, the three of them went into the kitchen and were talking with John and Joan, when they all heard a loud sound in the unoccupied family room. Shannon stated that it sounded "like a cannon had gone off --- it had that much force." They went to investigate and learned that a heavy bronze candlestick (which had been on the floor to the immediate left of the loveseat and near the back door) had taken flight a short distance and had banged into the door. That door, which was made of metal, was hit with such force that two dents were left on it. The Resch's had taken to placing heavy objects like this on the floor because it seemed that items left on walls and tables had a habit of flying in Tina's direction. Once, a wrought-iron clock had flown from the wall and had hit her in the back of the head, leaving a lump.

A few moments after the first, another bronze candlestick took flight from the other side of the loveseat, near the kitchen. Tina was sitting in a chair in the family room and Shannon and Harden were watching her from a couch across the room. No one was anywhere near the candle holder and yet somehow, it moved! It all happened so fast, and the thing moved with such speed, that Shannon never even saw it start to go! According to Tina, who had been at an angle to see the candlestick, it had flown four of five feet into the kitchen before making a 90-degree turn and shooting down the hallway. She said that it had been turning end over end through the air.

Shannon admitted that he had not seen the candlestick, but he had certainly heard it. As it propelled itself, the object made a roaring sound, an incredible noise that he said sounded "something like a locomotive".

Everyone was shocked and when they recovered, they all got to their feet and hurried into the hallway. The first thing they saw was the hanging lamp at the entrance of the doorway. The lamp was swinging back and forth quite rapidly from what Shannon believed was wind left behind by the fast moving candlestick. The lamp, he later reported, was swinging as if it were in a hurricane.

The incident with the candlestick was only one of the strange things that happened while Harden and Shannon were watching Tina in the family room. Most of the other incidents involved telephones that were located on a stand next to Tina's chair. Many people have wondered why the Resch's had more than one phone on the stand. The reason for this was that when the outbreak began, the house was plagued with all sorts of electrical problems, including malfunctions with the telephone in the family room. Because of this, the Resch's bought a second, cheap phone and installed it next to the sturdier, original phone. Both sat on the stand next to the chair in the family room but it was the second phone that was most affected by the "force" in the house.

According to Fred Shannon, he was present on seven different occasions when one or the other of the phones flew in Tina's direction. The first two times, they hit her on the left side and fell next to her on the couch. During the other incidents, the phones flew over Tina's lap in the direction of the loveseat. The events occurred unexpectedly, usually minutes apart, but happened in seconds. This made it nearly impossible for Shannon to get a photograph of the events. At one point, he sat for more than 20 minutes with the camera up to his eye, wait-

ing for some-
thing to hap-
pen - but
nothing did.
Finally, each
time that he
would lower
the camera so
that he wasn't
immediately
ready to take
a photo ---
the phone
would go fly-
ing through
the air!

The photo that was taken by Fred Shannon while at the Resch house. It later went on to be picked upBy the Associated Press and appeared in newspapers all over the country. Skeptics would attempt to debunk the photo, even going as far as to smear Shannon's upstanding reputation, in order to prove their point.
(photo Associated Press / Columbus Dispatch)

That caused him to wonder if he was dealing with a blind force after all. Could it be aware of his presence? If this was true, he decided to devise a strategy. He brought the camera to his eye, his finger poised on the trigger, and waited, watching Tina for about five minutes. Then, without taking his eyes off her, he lowered the camera to the level of his waist, still keeping it pointed in her direction and his finger on the shutter. As he did this, he turned his head in the direction of the kitchen, where the Resch's were talking with some visitors. He waited patiently for something to happen, pretending that his attention was somewhere else.

A few seconds later, he saw a white blur out of the corner of his eye and by the time that he pressed the shutter of the camera, a phone had streaked through the air and had sailed all the way across the chair in which Tina was sitting! The resulting photo captured not only the flying telephone but also the frightened expression on Tina's face as she jerked backwards to keep from being hit. In all, Shannon was able to get three different photos of the telephone in flight but this first one was the one that got the most attention. The day after it appeared in the local newspaper, it was picked up by the Associated Press and made front pages all over the country.

The photo was immediately attacked by the debunkers, who began savaging the entire case, but Shannon was adamant about what he had seen. He empha-

94

sized in writing: "I am damned sure that she did not throw those phones. From what Mike and I observed, I would say that she couldn't possibly have thrown them - absolutely no way. We were sitting in a well-lighted room; we were looking right at her. When one of us was looking away for a moment, the other had his eyes on Tina all the time. And of course, there were some objects that took flight while she was nowhere near them - the candlesticks, for example."

Shannon also witnessed an incident with the telephones that did not involve Tina. It occurred just a few minutes after Shannon took the astounding photo of the phone in flight. A Franklin County Children Services caseworker and an associate arrived at the house on business and the caseworker sat down in the loveseat. Shannon warned her not to sit there as he knew that she would be in a direct path of the telephone. She didn't take him seriously and made several comments to assure him that she thought the whole thing was a joke, but humored him anyway by moving to the other cushion on the loveseat. She stood up, shuffled sideways and sat back down again. Just as she was lowering herself to the seat, the phone shot through the air and landed hard on the cushion where she had been sitting. If she had not moved, the phone would have struck her in the chest! The incident startled her so much that she made no more light of it and she and her co-worker quickly finished their business and left.

A little while later, Harden, Shannon and Tina were standing in the middle of the family room when a box of tissues (which was also on the phone table) suddenly leapt into the air. It zipped past Shannon's leg and landed on a small table next to the couch. When it hit the table, it did not skip or bounce even though it had been moving at tremendous speed. Instead, it stopped in place as if it had been caught by a magnet or glued into position.

This was the last activity that Shannon witnessed in the family room but his experiences at the Resch house were not yet over. He decided to take some photos in the kitchen and hoped that if he got Tina to open the refrigerator door, something would fly out of it, as had been allegedly happening over the last few days. The kitchen was already a mess from these past incidents and in fact, the Resch's had been cleaning the room during most of the time that Shannon and Harden had been in the house.

Tina waited in the kitchen as he set up his camera in the corner, directly across the room from the refrigerator. Shannon ducked low to avoid being hit by any flying food and asked Tina to open the door --- but nothing happened. She repeated it three times but everything inside remained where it was. Tina decided to use the moments of inactivity to make a sandwich and Harden and Shannon decided to pack up and leave, having spent nearly four hours in the house.

As soon as the story of the Resch house, and Shannon's accompanying photo, began to appear in newspapers, the self-appointed critics of the paranormal immediately began an attack on the reality of the events that were being reported. In spite of the fact that none of them had investigated the case, nor had been to Columbus, they were convinced that the whole thing was a hoax. It was simply a matter of "if I don't believe it, then there is no way that it can be true".

The debunkers managed to obtain the negatives of the photos that Fred Shannon had shot at the house. Because there were three photos of a phone in the air above Tina's lap (not just the one that appeared in AP wire stories), Shannon was immediately accused of faking the photos and having Tina throw the phone so that he could photograph it. Although Shannon explained how he managed to capture three photos, he was dismissed as a fraud. This was done without investigation of the scene, assessment of the evidence and with no regard to Shannon's 30-year career and outstanding reputation.

The debunkers also dismissed the entire case based on the fact that Dr. Roll admitted that he believed that Tina had faked some of the less impressive activity in the house. However, he did believe that genuine activity was taking place in the case, even when conceding there was some limited fraud involved as well. "It is certain that Tina threw a lamp down on one occasion," he said. "That's obvious. She told me that she did the same thing on two other occasions. So there's no doubt there were some fraudulent occurrences."

Roll stated that it was not uncommon for victims of poltergeists to get into the act themselves as part of the mischief-making. He had been able to formulate many of the poltergeist patterns into a profile through his research. Usually at the center of the activity was a child or teenager who possessed a great deal of internal anger, usually caused by a stressful situation in the household or a mental disturbance. The PK was an unconscious, and unknowing, way of venting that hostility without fear of punishment. Because of the mental states of the agents in many of his cases, genuine phenomena and trickery often go hand in hand.

In such cases, the PK effects of the unstable person will actually cause genuine phenomena to occur. However, as the events are recorded and gain the attention of others in the household (and sometimes even the authorities and media), the agent in the case begins to receive the much-needed attention they desired. As this begins to occur, the phenomena will cease. To continue the attention, the agent will often fake the phenomena. Unfortunately, as the agent is often caught in the act of doing this, debunkers will claim the entire case was a hoax and are able to discredit any research material gathered in the early stages of the case. Because of this, many authentic cases are never brought to public record.

Roll felt that the minor episodes that occurred did not discredit the Resch case. "I can only say that when I was present, I couldn't find any ordinary explanation for the incidents I witnessed," he stated. "In my opinion, it is very unlikely that they were caused normally. And of course there are a number of witnesses we interviewed in Columbus who had seen things under conditions where no family members could have caused them."

Later that month, Roll took Tina back to North Carolina where he and other scientists conducted computer-based ESP and PK tests on her. The results of the test were in no way striking, leading most to believe that she did not possess any long-term psychic abilities. As in other poltergeist cases, the mysterious happenings seemed to be confined to a short period of time. And while there were some poltergeist incidents in the home of Dr. Roll and at the home of a counselor where Tina was staying, the researchers believed that her aggressive manipulations were short-lived.

What caused the manifestations? No one knows for sure and the story behind the Columbus poltergeist remains a mystery. Poltergeists in general tend to focus on disturbed children who are suppressing hostility and anger. The displacement of energy acts as a safety valve for the pent-up emotions. In Tina's case, there had been recent problems at home over the fact that Tina, against the wishes of John and Joan, had recently been searching for her natural parents. Also, Tina's best friend of two years had ended their friendship just two days before the events began. To make matters worse, the Resch's had recently taken Tina out of school because she was having trouble getting along with other students. She was apparently unpopular with most of her classmates and was having difficulty with one of her teachers. Because of this, she was being tutored at home and was seemingly "cut off" from the outside world. All of this apparently combined to create an outward transference of energy.

Eventually, the activity ended and after Tina's return from North Carolina, only a few minor incidents were reported in the home. Dr. Roll was never sure of the cause of the case, but his studies pointed to the theory that poltergeist agents seemed to suffer from disturbances in the central nervous system. This may have been the case with Tina Resch, for even though the bizarre incidents ended in her home, her story was not quite over.

Many poltergeist agents have been documented to be in poor mental health, which deteriorated further in stressful situations. This might explain the findings of many standard psychologists and mental health professionals. They often discover that patients with unresolved emotional issues are associated with, or have lived in, houses where poltergeist activity has been reported. In addition, while studying the personalities of those thought to be poltergeist agents, psychologists have found anxiety issues, phobias, mania, obsessions, dissociative disorders and even schizophrenia. In some cases, psychotherapy may eliminate the poltergeist phenomena but apparently, not in all of them.

For despite counseling, Tina Resch went from being an unhappy child to being a disturbed adult. She went from one disastrous situation to another, finally to two marriages and two divorces and then finally to a sentence of life in prison for the torture murder of her own daughter. Although she claimed to be innocent of the crime, she was sent to a Georgia prison in 1994 and remains there today.

By the late 1920's, many psychical investigators had turned from the investigation of spirit mediums to the study of haunted houses, churches and other buildings that were said to be inhabited by ghosts. One of the foremost researchers of the day was Harry Price, a man who set many of the standards for the modern ghost hunter. Around 1929, Price put together what he called his "ghost hunter's kit" and one of the main pieces of equipment for the kit was a camera, which would be used along with flash bulbs and film. Price compiled this list of gear for his ground-breaking, year-long investigation of a crumbling manor house called Borley Rectory. At the place that became known as "the most haunted house in England", Price made liberal use of the camera, photographing the exterior and the interior of the house, the occupants of the home and many of the participants in the investigation and dramatically, mysterious and unexplained writings that appeared on the walls of the rectory. A number of years later, after the rectory was burned, a photograph that was taken of the ruins seemed to show a brick that levitated out of the rubble and was suspended in the air.

Harry Price

Price's fascination with the camera came from his interest in photography and the debunking that he did of many spirit photography "mediums", who used questionable techniques to fool their clients into believing that the spirits of their loved ones were appearing on film with them. Even earlier than that though, Price began using cameras in his investigations of haunted houses, including the first investigation that he ever conducted.

That first investigation was carried out when Price was still in school. He and a young friend obtained permission to spend the night in an old manor house that was rumored to be haunted. The house had been purchased by a retired canon of the Church of England and his wife and within a few weeks of their settling in, reports of curious happenings began in the stable and out buildings. Though fastened securely overnight, stable doors were found open in the morning, animals were discovered wandering loose, pans of milk were overturned and utensils scattered about. Piles of logs in the woodshed were found tossed about in the morning, even though the door had been securely locked. These problems in the woodshed became so frequent and troublesome that it was decided that someone would keep watch on it. This was done on several occasions with one of the farm hands hiding behind piles of logs. However, nothing happened inside of the shed on those nights. Instead, small rocks began to be thrown onto the tin roof of the structure and could plainly be heard as they rattled off and fell to the ground. When watch was kept inside and outside of the shed, no one saw anything and yet the rocks were still heard falling.

The disturbances around the house continued but then quite suddenly, they stopped and the activities outside began to occur inside of the manor house.

The manor house, which was quite ancient but had been restored several times, was described as a very comfortable old house. From the large hall, a wide staircase led upstairs from the landing and at the top of the stairs was an oak gate that had been fitted to keep the resident dogs from roaming all over the house. The first indication by the canon and his family that something odd was now happening in the house were the soft "pattering" sounds of children's feet running up and down the wide gallery at the top of the stairs. The noises were first thought to be a small animal or something but an investigation turned up nothing. The noises were heard night after night and shortly after, the maids began complaining that pots, pans and utensils in the kitchen were being disturbed. Pans fell off the shelves for no reason, often when a maid was just a few feet away but with her back turned. Items also began to vanish without explanation and soon the entire household was in an uproar. The canon, who was already in declining health, began to suffer from sleepless nights caused by the strange activity, which by now was growing even worse. The small tapping of children's feet had been replaced by a steady thumping, as if someone with heavy boots was stomping around the place. The canon was soon persuaded to leave the house on a short holiday.

As it happened, Price was on his way back to school and stopped in the village to visit some friends. They told him about the weird goings-on at the manor house and his interest was immediately piqued. The canon and his household had temporarily vacated the house and left the place in the care of a worker and his wife. Price decided to try and get permission to stay the night in the house and invited one of his friends to join him. He later said that the caretaker's wife, who readily agreed to their request, must have "regarded us as a couple of mad schoolboys who would have been much better in bed".

In those days, Price had little idea as to what equipment needed to be taken along on a ghost investigation but one thing that he knew he needed was his Lancaster stand camera. On the day of his adventure, he rode his bicycle into town and purchased some magnesium powder, a bell switch, a roll of flex wire, two batteries and some sulphuric acid. He assembled his batteries and switch and prepared the flash powder as he planned to hopefully photograph "something" at the house. To make sure that the powder flashed at the time that he wanted, he mixed the gunpowder from several shotgun cartridges in with the magnesium powder. He used the wire to hook up an electrical circuit to ignite the powder. With these implements, a box of matches, some candles, a lantern, a piece of chalk, a ball of string, a box of photographic plates, some food and the camera and accessories, Price and his companion said goodbye to their friends and made their way across the fields to the manor house. They arrived there just after darkness had fallen.

The first thing they did when they reached the house was to search every room and the attic and to close and fasten every window. They locked the doors of all of the rooms and then removed the keys. The doors leading into the house were all locked, barred and bolted and chairs and small items of furniture were placed in front of them. In this way, they determined that not only was the house empty, but there was no way that anyone could gain entry to the place. The two young men then locked themselves into a small parlor and waited for something to happen. Their only illumination was the small lantern, which they placed on a table.

At about 11:30, Price and his friend were beginning to get tired when suddenly, his companion said that he heard a noise in a room overhead. Price had also heard a noise but had dismissed it as nothing more than a rodent or the wind. A few minutes later though, there was a "thud" in the room that could not have been anything other than someone walking around. It was followed by what sounded like someone stumbling over a chair. Realizing that they were not alone in the house, the two boys were "paralyzed with fear" but braced their nerves and waited to see what happened next.

Just before midnight, they heard noises again. This time, it seemed to be someone in heavy boots, stomping around the room. A minute or so later, the footsteps apparently left the room and began walking across the upstairs gallery. They paused for a moment at the top of the stairs and then began to descend. The young men counted 15 distinct steps, the same number as the stairs, and then the footsteps paused for a moment as if wondering which way to go next.

"The fact that only a door intervened between us and the mysterious intruder made us take a lively interest in what its move would be," Price wrote many years later. "We were not kept long in suspense. The entity, having paused in the hall for about three minutes, turned tail and stomped up the stairs again, every step being plainly heard."

The mysterious footsteps stopped at the gate at the top of the staircase and then no more sound came. Price and his friend waited at the door for a few minutes more and then decided to investigate. They had just reached this decision when they heard the footsteps turn and start to descend the staircase again. They counted the footsteps as they came closer and closer, listened as they paused for a moment in the hall and then started back up the steps again.

The two young men were growing ever bolder and now decided to take a look at who, or what, was on the stairs. Price grabbed his camera and opened the door. His friend followed close behind with the lantern. By this time, the footsteps were on the fifth stair and when the door of the parlor creaked open, they immediately stopped.

Price wrote: "Realizing that the ghost was as frightened of meeting us as we were of seeing it (although that is what we had come for), we thought we would again examine the stairs and the upper part of the house. This we did very thoroughly, but found nothing disturbed. The dog-gate was still latched and tied with string. To this day I am wondering whether 'it' climbed over the gate (easily accomplished by a mortal), or whether it slipped through the bars. I think we were disappointed at not seeing anything we could photograph, so decided to make an attempt at a flashlight picture if the poltergeist would descend the stairs again."

Price began searching for something that he could use as a stand for his flash powder and eventually tracked down a short household ladder from the kitchen. He opened the ladder and placed it about 12 feet from the bottom of the staircase. On top of it, he heaped a large pile of his gunpowder and magnesium powder mixture and then wired it up with the battery that he had purchased. The wires ran from the staircase and into the parlor, where he hooked them up to the bell switch and prepared to fire off the flash from this spot.

After some thought, Price decided to try and photograph the source of the footsteps as it was climbing up the stairs. By the light of a match, Price focused his camera, inserted a plate, uncapped the lens and then placed the camera on the steps. After getting everything arranged, the boys hurried back into the parlor and locked the door. Then they lay down on the carpet near the door and with the trigger in hand, continued their vigil.

Nearly an hour passed before they heard anything and once again, it came from the room over their heads. The sounds were the same as what they had heard earlier. Shortly after, the thumps could be heard approaching the gate and then pausing at the top of the stairs. The pause lasted for several minutes and then started down the steps again. When the sound reached the bottom, it stopped again. Price tried to mentally visualize where the "ghost" might be standing. In order to get the camera square with the steps, he had used a large book to balance it, then had drawn a chalk line on the tiled floor to run parallel with the stairs. The line could be used as a marker to photograph whatever might be there and he tried to imagine whether the footsteps were in position.

Several minutes passed with no movement in the hallway. Then, the "ghost" started its return journey up the stairs. With their hearts beating wildly, the boys lay on the floor counting the steps as they ascended the staircase. At the seventh thump, Price pushed the button on the switch and the flash powder exploded in the hallway. The light was so bright that even the parlor was lit up by the illumination that came from under the door.

At the same moment as the explosion, the "ghost" was so startled that it involuntarily stumbled on the stairs, a sound the boys could plainly hear. After that, there was silence, followed by a clattering sound as if the entity had fallen down.

"It was difficult to say who was the more startled," Price later recalled, "the poltergeist or myself, and for some moments we did nothing."

After the young men got over their astonishment, they opened the door and found the hallway filled with a white smoke that was so dense they could hardly breathe. They re-lit their lantern, re-capped and grabbed the camera. The boys immediately developed the plate but unfortunately, the over-exposed picture of the staircase --- and perhaps a ghost --- was nothing but a washed out negative.

As years have passed, many advances have been made in both photography and paranormal investigation. In recent times, new theories have been developed which seem to suggest that many haunted locations have high levels of electromagnetic energy present in them. Many believe that ghost themselves may be electromagnetic in origin or perhaps that the ghosts actually use this energy to manifest. Whatever the answer, researchers began adapting electronic devices as a way to detect the energy that was not visible to the human eye. There are theories that exist to say that the energy a ghost gives off, or uses, whether it is a conscious spirit or residual energy, causes a disruption in the magnetic field of the location and thus, becomes detectable using measuring devices --- and on some occasions, perhaps with a camera as well.

Today, even the most inexperienced ghost hunter is familiar with the use of electromagnetic field detectors but for many years, the only devices that could be used to measure energy changes were Geiger counters, which measure levels of radiation.

Geiger counters were really first acknowledged as useful in the paranormal field in 1974, when the "Entity" case began. Researchers Barry Taff and Kerry Gaynor from the now defunct Department of Parapsychology at UCLA, became involved in a haunting that would go on to be the basis for a book and film, as well as for years of study and speculation.

According to the woman who was embroiled at the center of the case, her home was haunted and she was being repeatedly attacked and raped by the spirits that were present. Taff and Gaynor spent many hours documenting the reported events and speaking to witnesses who had seen apparitions in the house but became concerned that "Doris", as she was dubbed, was either crazy or making things up. They did not plan to pursue the case at all.

However, a few days later, Doris called and informed them that five individuals outside of her family had now seen the apparitions. So Taff and Gaynor decided to return to the house with cameras and tape recorders. They immediately noticed something odd when they entered Doris' bedroom. Even though it was a hot, August night and the windows were closed, the temperature was unusually low when compared to the rest of the house. The cold spots faded in and out irregularly, sometimes completely disappearing. They could find no source for the cold areas, but these anomalies would not be the only methods through which the phenomena would make itself known.

The first of many inexplicable happenings occurred while Gaynor was talking to Doris' oldest son in the kitchen. He was standing a short distance from a lower kitchen cabinet when the cabinet door suddenly swung open and a pan jumped out of it, landing about three feet away.

After examining the cabinet, Taff and Gaynor went into the bedroom with Doris and her friend, Candy, who had joined them for the evening and who purported to be psychic. Taff took a photograph of the bedroom with a Polaroid SX-70 camera and it came out perfectly. After they were in the room for about 15 minutes, Candy shouted that she sensed something in the corner. Taff ran back into the room with the camera and immediately aimed and fired it in that direction.

The photograph that resulted was bleached completely white, as if it had been exposed to some sort of intense energy or radiation. The same thing happened a few minutes later when Candy again directed their attention to the corner. This time, the photo still bleached out, but not as badly as the first time. Puzzled, Taff took another photo (thinking that something might be wrong with the camera) but this time in the living room. This photo came out fine, as did subsequent photos taken by Kerry Gaynor in the bedroom. The only difference was that these photos were not taken while Candy "sensed" something else in the room with them.

A short time later, Taff took another photo, this time because of a cold breeze that came from the closed bedroom door. This photo turned out to be the strangest of the night, showing a ball of light that was about one foot in diameter. It hovered a few inches from the door in the photo, but no one had actually seen the light appear.

Moments later, while the investigators were poring over the photo, Taff happened to glance over toward the bedroom's east window. In a flash, he spotted several rapidly moving blue balls of light. He immediately raised the Polaroid camera and took a picture in the direction of the curtains. The resulting photo was blurred and badly bleached but the blue lights that Taff had seen were nowhere to be found.

A few minutes later, Candy again warned about the presence of an entity in the room, this time standing directly in front of her. Taff fired the Polaroid in her direction and he obtained an odd photo of Candy. Her face was completely bleached out, yet her dress and the room behind and around her was completely clear and distinct. Another photo, this time taken by Kerry Gaynor under the same conditions, again captured Candy with bleaching about her face while the rest of the photograph was again very clear.

At this point, they became convinced that something out of the ordinary was occurring in the house.

Over the course of the next ten weeks, a team from UCLA was almost always present in the house. They returned many times for investigations, bringing dozens of eyewitnesses, researchers and photographers with them. Initially, most of the researchers were skeptical of the events reported by Taff and Gaynor but soon, more of them began to share their belief of the happenings after wit-

The famous photo taken during the "Entity" Case that would late appear as "unexplained" in Popular Mechanics Magazine. (Barry Taff)

nessing them for themselves.

One night, what can only be described as a "light show" took place in the house in front of 20 startled onlookers. However, most of the photos that were taken of them were disappointing. The light was so bright that most of them came out overexposed. One photo though, did manage to show what the investigators saw that night. The frame was filled with reverse arcs of light. The reason this photo was so important is that the arc on the wall, if it were really on the wall, would be bent because the two walls are perpendicular to each other. In the photo however, the arc is not bent, which means that it was floating in space at the time and signifies that it was dimensional and not just a flashlight being aimed at the wall.

One of the witnesses present that night was Frank De Felitta, an author who would go on to write a book based on the case. De Felitta would later vividly recall the light as it moved into the center of the room and the shouts from those present. He said that Doris started screaming as the light moved toward her, cursing and daring the entity to show itself, instead of just a light. At that point, it started to appear and witnesses would later claim to see a part of an arm, a neck and what looked like a bald head. Everyone present saw the same thing at the same time, ruling out any individual's hallucinations.

Another interesting event of the evening involved an extremely sensitive Geiger counter that had been brought along to record any activity in the radiation field of the house. The instrument began behaving very oddly when the lights were the most active as the previously constant background radiation registering on the device dropped off to zero. When the light activity began to dwindle and then fade away, the Geiger counter's meter returned to its normal level of ambient background radiation. Barry Taff believed that it was possible that the strange activity either used the background radiation as an energy source or that the energy given off by the lights scattered the ambient energy field in such a way that it could no longer be registered.

Over the next few weeks, the activity continued but that strange night seemed to be the climax of the events. The phenomena began to diminish little by little and although there were more violent episodes, even after Doris and her family left the house, they were never as strong as they had once been.

The photograph that was taken showing the weird "arc" of light in the room was later featured in *Popular Mechanics* magazine and remains unexplained to this day.

PHOTOGRAPHY IN PARANORMAL INVESTIGATIONS

Today, there are few paranormal researchers who are using their cameras to document the phenomena created by Spiritualist mediums. Most of us are putting our efforts towards using the camera to document not only ghosts but the strange happenings that sometimes occur during our investigations of haunted locations. As in the case of researchers like Harry Price, we are hoping that the camera will capture something truly incredible during the course of the investigation --- and in some cases, it does.

In the pages ahead, we will take a closer look at how cameras can provide legitimate evidence in paranormal research, as well as some ideas about conducting paranormal investigations and the best uses for your camera during these outings.

When conducting investigations, remember that photographing ghosts is not an easy process. Many investigators only use a camera when they encounter anomalous readings with their equipment and still others cover the location with their camera to document as much as they can. You just never know what might turn up on your developed film. Do plan to use a lot of film when you are ghost hunting. It is a common fact that it sometimes takes dozens (or even hundreds) of snapshots to come up with even one paranormal photo that you can feel is genuine. With this being the case, try not to get discouraged if every investigation fails to turn up a "ghost photo". Just because you don't get any results with your camera, doesn't mean the location is not haunted. The camera is just like any other tool in your ghost hunting kit. The results that you achieve with it do not stand alone and it's always possible that you won't find anything with your camera, even though your other equipment says that something is there.

And when the camera does work, you still have to be careful. Turning to the camera for proof of ghosts does not insure against mistakes and many ghost hunters are fooled into believing that some erroneous photos are real. We have all seen dozens of photos that supposedly show ghosts and paranormal energy but that actually do not. Be careful to do your research and know how to tell "accidental" photos from the real thing. Here are some things to be careful of when experimenting with ghost photographs:

1. Be careful that you have nothing protruding in front of the camera lens. Believe it or not, this can be anything from a finger to clothing, items around you like trees, grass, solid objects, clothing and even hair. People with long hair should make sure that it is pulled back tightly or tucked under a hat. Loose hair that ends up in front of the camera lens (which may be unseen by the photographer) and which gets illuminated by the flash can look pretty eerie.

2. Be sure that your lens is clean and covered when not in use. Even a small drop of rain, dirt or moisture that ends up on the lens can show up on the developed print. This would not be seen through the viewfinder, so you would never know that it was there.

3. Make sure the weather is cooperating with your photographs. By this, I mean to make sure that it is not raining or snowing. Round balls of glowing light that are photographed during a rain storm are not exactly overwhelming proof of the supernatural.

4. Make sure that conditions are not damp, promoting moisture or fogging, on your camera lens. This is why I always mention bringing along temperature and humidity gauges to an investigation site. You can check and see if "fog-like" images that later turn up on film could have a natural explanation.

5. Be sure to point the camera away from reflective surfaces when using a flash. Avoid mirrors and windows in a house and bright or polished surfaces when working outdoors. The light from the flash bouncing off this surface can refract back onto your camera lens and create "orbs" that are not of paranormal origins. This can often happen in cemeteries with reflective tombstones, especially polished granite, which easily catch the light.

6. Make sure you know where your camera strap is at all times. Notice how many so-called "ghost photos" that you see look like camera straps? That's because most of them are! Notice how those "anomalous" images always come from the right side of the camera, where the strap is normally located? I suggest taking the strap off your camera or at least leaving it around your neck, where it belongs.

7. No matter where you are taking photographs, be sure to use a photographic log sheet to keep track of where the photos were taken, who took them and whether or not they were taken randomly or because some strange activity was occurring at the time. This can be very important when it comes to analyzing the photos and looking for corresponding activity at the site.

USING 35MM CAMERAS IN GHOST HUNTING

Ghost hunters that I meet around the country often ask me to suggest cameras and film for paranormal investigations but there really doesn't seem to be a definitive type of either one to use. I have seen remarkable photos that have been taken with everything from expensive 35mm cameras to instant cameras to even cheap, disposable cameras. Obviously, cost is almost always a determining factor in choosing a camera, but remember that while an $800 camera may be of a better quality than a $200 one, it is the person behind the lens who makes all the difference, unless you are dealing with a digital camera and then technology is almost as important as the person using the equipment.

There are many different kinds of cameras manufactured today but the most popular 35mm cameras are two basic types. One of them is the "point and shoot" camera, which is very simple and is completely automatic in its operation. The other camera type is the Single Lens Reflex camera (SLR). This type can be more complex to operate but is a favorite for most professional and amateur photographers. I usually recommend to people that they use a model of camera that is most comfortable for them, regardless of the type. When it comes to film, I usually suggest Kodak 400 ASA film (and sometimes higher speeds) for overnight, outdoor investigations, depending on the strength of your camera flash. There are three basic methods of photography to consider when photographing your investigations:

COLOR FILM: This is the simplest and most basic method of photography during both daytime and nighttime investigations. For interior locations, or daytime investigations, use a 200 ASA Kodak film. At night, I would recommend a 400 ASA speed Kodak film, along with your camera flash, to obtain results. This is a small grain film, so enlargements will not be difficult and it is fast enough to use under low light conditions. You may want to experiment with your camera at night and make sure this is a high enough speed film for your particular model of camera.

BLACK & WHITE FILM (No Flash): If you prefer to try and experiment without the flash, thus eliminating the chance for false orbs and lens refractions, you will want to use a 400 ASA film made by Tri-X or Kodak. This film is ideal because it is more sensitive to ultraviolet light and so you have a better chance of possibly picking up something unseen by the human eye. In most cases, the Kodak film can be developed by just about any processor but it should be developed at the same settings as color film, so be sure that your processor is aware of this.

INFRARED FILM: One of the most reliable, but most difficult to use, types of film and photography is infrared. There is a lot of experimentation and money involved with using it but this type of film is sensitized to light that we can see with the naked eye, as well as light that is of a different wavelength of radiation and is invisible to us. The film allows you to see, literally, what is beneath the surface, or what the human eye cannot see. Infrared does not detect heat, but rather sees and photographs radiation. It can actually "see" a level of radiation that is one spectrum below thermal radiation and this is radiation caused by electromagnetic fields. Because we believe that paranormal energy also lurks in this same "dead zone", infrared film becomes a very helpful tool in ghost hunting.

However, infrared film does require special filters to use, must always be kept refrigerated, requires special processing and must always be loaded and unloaded into the camera under conditions of absolute darkness. Also, most automatic cameras cannot be used with infrared film. There in an infrared sensor inside most models to make sure that the film advances properly. This sensor will badly cloud your film.

The Best Way to Use Infrared Film:

1. It has been suggested that if you are going to try infrared film, you should

take along 2 different cameras on an investigation. One of them should be loaded with 400 (or higher) ASA film and one with infrared film. Your local camera shop should be able to order it for you, or you can order it directly from Kodak for about $12 per roll. Always ask for HIE 135 Black & White film. It comes in 36 exposure rolls.

Remember that you are going to have to experiment with this film. The first time that you use it may be a total bust! Make sure that you make notes for each exposure that you take about your camera settings so that you will know later what worked and what didn't. I suggest making your first trip out to a place where you don't expect activity, just so that you know how the film works best with your camera. There is always time later for a solid investigation using infrared film.

2. When the film arrives, it should have come in a box packed in dry ice to keep it cool. This is essential for Infrared film is sensitive to heat and must be kept refrigerated before it is used. If you buy the film (already in stock) at the camera shop, make sure that it was kept cool. You should store the film inside of your refrigerator and not take it out until about one hour before you are going to load it into your camera. This way, it warms to room temperature and you avoid any chance of fogging on the film.

3. Also essential is the fact that this film must be loaded and unloaded in total darkness. Find a room or a closet with no outside light and stuff towels under the door or any other way that will make the room pitch dark. Then, you can safely load the film into your camera. Any light leaks at all can damage the film.

4. When using the film, some researchers recommend different filters to use when working with infrared film, so experiment and see what works best for you. Deep red filter blocks (no. 25) will block out visible light if you want that. When shooting in the daylight, you will want to make sure that you have a filter, as UV rays and other spectrums of light can cloud or overexpose the film. Also, try not to use a flash because you can get some very weird light reflections from it. It's best to just open up your lens to the widest aperture and experiment with it. If you do use a flash, be sure that it has the same type of filter over it that your lens does.

5. After the film is exposed, unload it in the "dark room" you created and place it back into the container that it came in. Tape the canister shut and do not allow it to be opened by anyone until it is ready to be processed.

DIGITAL CAMERAS & GHOST HUNTING

When I first began writing about ghost hunting and published my first research manual on the subject in 1997, I was already speaking out against digital cameras and why they should not be used for paranormal research. However, one of the statements that I made was that perhaps someday the technology of the digital camera would finally be adaptable to the sort of studies that legitimate researchers would like to do. And, after all of this time, it looks as though that day has finally arrived. I still feel that standard cameras are essential for paranormal research but I also feel that digital cameras do have a place as well.

After my first book on ghost hunting was published, I began to be under constant and continued attack for my stance against digital cameras. Many of those who criticized my opinion misunderstood the point, believing that I had something against the cameras themselves. This was not the case. I always understood the benefits of them. They provided instant images, there was no wasted film or development costs. In most cases, you could actually see the photo in a matter of seconds after it was taken. I understood the reasoning behind this. Digital cameras were saving ghost hunters a lot of money but I could never just accept the authenticity of the images that were photographed by them.

No matter what I ever said or wrote though, digital cameras continued to be used in ghost research. Thankfully, not all ghost hunters were using them incorrectly. These cameras have always been excellent for documenting a location and also as a secondary, back-up camera. The problem came when the digital cameras were the only cameras used in an investigation. This was (and still is) an incorrect use for the camera and it has led to some disastrous results for the credibility of paranormal investigations. Many ghost hunters are out snapping hundreds of digital photos at random, using nothing else for their "investigation" but the camera. They are presenting digital images as absolute proof of the paranormal and by doing so, are making a mockery out of the real investigations that are going on. Fortunately, these people are in the minority when it comes to paranormal investigators, but they are still out there, wreaking havoc with their cameras.

But why was I so concerned about digital cameras and why would I maintain for more that six years that they should not be used in paranormal research?

Earlier in this book, I mentioned the problem that the early digital cameras had when operating under low-light conditions. I have always referred to this as the "orb factor" and it was an ongoing problem with digital photography for years. There were a great number of ghost hunters who were out on "investigations" and discovering copious amounts of "orbs" in their photos. Unfortunately, they were nothing more than sections of the images where the pixels did not fill in completely. The good news is that time and advances in digital technology have all but eliminated this problem in the newer and better quality cameras. The lingering problems come from those who have not updated their cameras for newer models and we'll discuss that in a moment.

Aside from the "orb" problems in the older digital cameras, the biggest problem that was being experienced was that there was no way to determine if an image was genuine or not. To be able to analyze a photo and to be able to determine the photo's authenticity, two things have always been needed --- a print of the photo and its negative. This was something that a digital camera could not provide and since electronic images taken with the older cameras could be easily altered and changed, it was impossible to prove they were authentic.

Time, and technology, has changed though and now it is not only possible to authenticate the images that have been taken with a digital camera but, depending on the camera, it can be used as the primary photographic instrument in an investigation.

In addition to trying to rule out natural explanations for reported activity before considering that it might be signs of a haunting, one of my other research philosophies has always been to try and continue to update my theories of the paranormal. I do not believe that we will ever know all that there is to know about this field and I have never stopped searching for further information. There is much that we still have to learn and even when it comes to something that I have been as adamant about as digital cameras, I am the first to admit when I have altered my theories based on new technology and new information.

My theories have only recently changed and I would still maintain that, prior to recent times, digital cameras have not been suitable for paranormal investigation. At no time have the older cameras been capable of collecting authentic evidence and I base this on the problems with the false "orbs" that the makers of the cameras readily admitted to and also because of the lack of a negative or any other method of examining a digital image in order to authenticate it. Until just recently, the authentication of digital images was only possible with professional quality digital cameras, which were far out of reach of the ordinary person. For this reason, only lower quality cameras were being used by investigators and strong evidence could not, and can not, be collected using them.

But times have changed. It is now within the means of investigators to purchase 5 megapixel and greater cameras. These newer cameras not only offer clean and crisp images that do not have the problems with false "orbs" but some models also offer "Night Shot" technology and all of them even offer a way to authenticate the images that is as trustworthy as a negative. One of the options of a higher quality camera is access to what are called Raw Data files. These files are uncompressed and unprocessed and an anomalous image that is examined using this option can actually be authenticated - perhaps with even more detail than in a photographic negative. In addition, the newer cameras also offer access to the EXIF information about images that are photographed. EXIF is data that is embedded into the image once it is taken. It contains everything about the camera that took the image, including camera settings, date and time the image was taken, if flash was used, the ISO settings and more. If anyone attempts to manipulate the image, the EXIF data holds this information too. In this way, a person trying to analyze a digital image will be able to see if it has been manipulated or not. If anyone attempts to alter the EXIF data, it will destroy the image. In this way, it becomes a "digital negative" of every picture that is taken.

With this new technology now within reach of the average person, digital photography has reached a level where I believe it is finally acceptable in paranormal research. By using cameras that start at a level of no less than 5 megapixels and taking advantage of all of the options available to us, we can actually gather evidence with our digital camera that is comparable to that of a 35 mm camera.

With all of this said however, I do not want this to be misinterpreted as a blanket endorsement of the way that digital cameras have been used in the past. Neither the methods, nor the low quality cameras that have been used, have a place in the research if used improperly. Even now, with all of the technology that we have available, no camera should be used as the single tool in an investigation. Reputable photographs should still be accompanied by good research and corresponding activity, whether the captured images can be authenticated or not.

USING VIDEO IN YOUR INVESTIGATIONS

While this book has dealt mainly with print and digital photography, it would be remiss of me not to make mention of the use of video cameras in an investigation. Most ghost hunters have started taking and setting up video cameras for every investigation that they go on. Also, thanks to the fact that many of the newer cameras are now fitted with infrared (or as Sony calls it "Nightshot") capabilities, we can shoot at a 0 lux setting that allows us to film in total and complete darkness. This innovation has allowed us to overcome the problems of the past, when video cameras were not useful in dark locations.

One of the main uses for a video camera in an investigation is to record your witness interviews. You might be surprised by what turns up on video over what you might record on an ordinary audiotape. Just the expression on someone's face, or their mannerisms, can often speak volumes about an event and bring to light facts that you may not have even considered. The only problem with this is that many witnesses (in my experience) are ill at ease in front of a camera. This can often make for a disjointed and nervous accounting of events.

You should try the video camera first and if this doesn't work, switch over to recording on audiotape instead.

Another advantage to the video camera is the ease with which you can document the location of the investigation. I always recommend that researchers draw up a map or chart of the location and note the various areas where phenomena have been reported. This is much easier to do if you have covered the entire area with your video camera too. Also, if you are writing the investigation up as a report, you can check your memory of the location by watching the video that you have recorded.

To most researchers though, the main reason to carry a video camera into an investigation is for the chance to capture some sort of paranormal phenomena on tape. Of course, the fact that video does seem to pick up anomalies may discredit some of the past theories that we have entertained about how still cameras manage to pick up ghosts. It has long been suggested that the camera will pick up paranormal energy because it is moving faster than we can actually see. If this is true, then how do we explain how video cameras manage to record strange images? The video camera acts more like the human eye, seeing things in real time and not frozen as they are with a still camera. Perhaps ghosts actually are in that other spectrum of light, who knows? Regardless, there have been a number of very authentic video tapes that have emerged showing strange shapes, mists and especially, speeding balls of light that don't seem to be explainable except as paranormal phenomena. They appear to be some of the same anomalies that have been captured by still cameras. This leads me to think that they are probably the same type of phenomena.

Many of these videotapes were shot under ordinary conditions while investigators were checking out reportedly haunted locations. Some were filmed randomly and others were done while certain areas were under surveillance, which is another great use for the video camera in your investigation. In fact, I always recommend the use of several video cameras for an investigation if possible. This allows us to monitor various sections of the location because we never know where activity might occur next. One of the cameras can be used to record the witness testimony, while the others can be used to thoroughly cover the location.

The grueling part of this will be that you have to be sure and watch everything that you have recorded. You never know when something might turn up. I would even suggest, if you have the capability, to watch the tape frame-by-frame. It is very possible that you might miss something on the general run-through. This will take a lot of extra time, but may be well worth it. In one case that I was involved in, the location seemed to be without activity until the films were watched one frame at a time. After that, we realized that it was actually a very active place.

In the past, there have been many problems with using video cameras at dark investigation sites. In the case of older VHS cameras, it was pretty well impossible to film after the sun went down without the use of a lot of extra light sources. As times have changed though, better quality cameras have become available and in fact, it is now possible to use a standard, commercial camera and film in total darkness with it.

This type of camera has been manufactured in several models by Sony and is outfitted with what they call "Nightshot" capabilities. This means that it can film at 0 lux, in total darkness. The camera has the ability to convert infrared light to a part of the spectrum that the human eye can see. You can actually see the light being emitted by the camera and it literally "paints" the dark location and converts it to an inverted white and green color. It is an extremely effective device and for several years after it came on the market, it had better capabilities than most broadcast cameras that were being used by television and documentary crews.

As mentioned earlier, some of the best evidence captured on video has been the mysterious balls of light that are filmed at many haunted locations. The lights are normally round and often give off a faint glow. They move independent of their surroundings and dart between people and objects at the location. No one knows for sure what these lights may be, but as of now, they have no explanation whatsoever.

If you happen to find something like this on your videotape, be careful to observe the object's movements and be sure that it is not some sort of dust particle or airborne pollen. There are several ways that assurances can be reached, including the fact that dust has a distinctive way of moving on camera and will usually drift rather aimlessly back and forth as it settles. Heavier natural objects will always fall straight down past the camera, following the laws of gravity. The anomalous lights will have a movement pattern all their own and will seem to have a purpose. They will not float side to side and may even interact with the investigators or the witnesses at the scene.

There are ways that you can be sure of what you have filmed though. All that is required is measuring every object that can be seen on camera with a measuring tape, using an inexpensive wind gauge and having a lot of patience.

When setting up a location to be monitored on video, you should first monitor the wind speed directly in front of any heating or air conditioning vents. After you have logged in the highest velocity speed from in front of the vent, you will be able to say with certainty that dust will not move faster than the air flow at the location unless someone walks in front of the video camera. Once this data is collected, measure the distance of everything that can be seen in front of the camera, including the size of the room. Log this information in your notes next to the data from the wind gauge.

You can also adapt this to use in outdoor investigations as well. Most of us avoid trying to use video in the summer months because of the chance of picking up flying insects, but with the right calculations, you can rule out natural explanations during this time of year as well. Simply follow the same steps of measuring items that are in the line of sight of the camera and then also place your wind gauge within view of the camera. That way, any changes in wind speed will be picked up in the video record and comparisons can be made next to any anomalies that are filmed.

Video moves at 30 frames per second, so if an object moves one inch between frames (this is why you need to know the distance of everything in the room in relation to the possible anomaly), then it's moving at 30 inches per second. When broken down, this would equate to about 1.7 miles per hour, which means that it could clearly be dust. However, if it was moving one foot between frames, it would be traveling at 20.4 miles per hour, which means that, unless it is an insect, it is not dust. In many cases, investigators have filmed anomalies moving much faster than this, sometimes as quickly as 60 (or more) miles per hour. Even the world's fastest flying insect (the Australian Dragonfly at 35 miles per hour) does not move that quickly and by having measurement and wind speed data from your investigation site, you can obtains some very reliable and authentic evidence of the unknown.

Remember that using a video camera is just like using any other device in the pursuit of the paranormal. It takes practice to be good at it and experimentation is essential. To be able to obtain good, authentic evidence using a video camera, you have to use the same sort of caution that you use with anything else. Be sure that you carefully review any evidence that you might have before presenting it to the public and proclaiming it genuine. We have all seen examples, just like with still photos, of sloppy research that shows images that are far from paranormal in origin.

THE INVESTIGATION: USING YOUR CAMERA IN GHOST RESEARCH

In the manual for ghost hunters that I wrote, I provided a number of checklists and suggestions for those who are conducting investigations into the paranormal. The how-to guidelines that follow are obviously not lists that will work for everyone and my suggestion is that the information from this book (and from The Ghost Hunter's Guidebook) be adapted by the individual researcher for his own investigations. Whether you choose to follow these guidelines or not is up to you, but if nothing else, I think they may offer you some pretty valuable starting points.

I should start out by saying that I believe investigations are best conducted with teams made up of 5-6 people. This allows you to thoroughly investigate the entire location (without tripping all over a large group) and to interview the witness and record their statements without the person feeling overwhelmed. A small group will also allow you to avoid the distractions that arise and complicate the investigation for researchers who attempt to work alone or with only one other person. Remember that working alone in a research investigation is not recommended. You should always have someone else along, if not for safety's sake, then to at least be there to corroborate any strange things that might occur. On the other hand, a large group is merely pointless, especially in someone's home, where things quickly become awkward and congested.

Here are the steps to follow in an investigation:

1. Arrive with skepticism. Don't go into a location looking for ghosts --- go in looking for a natural explanation and rule out everything until there is nothing left but ghosts.

2. Make sure that the witness understands what you are going to do at their house or location. Make sure that they realize this can be an intrusive process. The more comfortable that the witness is, the better the investigation will go.

3. Next, divide up the separate functions of the investigation among the team members. Decide who will be handling what aspects, who will be photographing, who will be videotaping, who will be using what equipment, etc.

4. Interview the witness in a secluded location with all of the team members present except one. This excluded person should be simply walking through the house making a layout drawing of the rooms and getting a general impression of the place. This person should also note every location where he finds, or feels, something out of the ordinary. His perceptions will be essential to the findings of the investigation because he will not have any idea of the witness testimony or where previous encounters have taken place. A particularly sensitive member of the team is best suited for this assignment.

5. The other team members should be interviewing the witness, or witnesses, about the events in the case. The questions should be asked by one interviewer at a time and all of the interview should be recorded on tape and, if possible, video. One team member should also be taking notes of everything that is said. It is essential to get all of the details of the case in this first interview.

6. After the interview, an additional team member should begin another scan of the house with detection equipment, also noting any strange locations that may come up using the equipment. Particular attention should be paid to those areas where the witness recalled an experience or sighting.

At this point, it is also a good idea to compare notes with the first investigator who walked through the house. Try and determine if any of the locations where this person noted something unusual match anything from the witness testimony or from the use of the detection equipment.

7. Another team member should make a photographic record of the site with his camera, documenting each of the locations, particularly the area where the witness reports seem to gravitate. Using a video camera, a team member should document the location in this manner also. These photographs may become very valuable as a record of the place and may also pick up something out of the ordinary as well.

8. If the phenomena occurs on a regular basis, or has a set pattern, you should obtain permission from the witness to do a surveillance of the area for an extended period. I like to refer to this as a "ghost watch", because it gets away from actual ghost hunting and becomes more of a "wait and see what happens" experience. In these situations, it benefits the researchers to come to the location, set up their monitoring equipment and then wait to see what they can record. This is where your cameras and video cameras become especially important to your research.

THE GHOST WATCH: USING YOUR CAMERAS

The type of investigation known as the "Ghost Watch", actually means just sitting around and waiting for something to happen. It is not your proactive type of ghost hunting and for this reason, it is often overlooked by researchers. In all honesty, I feel that sidestepping this part of the investigation (mostly because it is mind-numbingly boring at times) can be a huge mistake. And it's also imperative when dealing with what you believe is a human agent poltergeist case.

The idea of the "ghost watch" comes into play when the ghost research team has become relatively sure that they cannot explain away the reports of the witnesses at the location. It can also be planned when the ghost hunter's investigations have turned up something beyond the ordinary. In these situations, the investigation veers away from interviewing witnesses and scanning with equipment and becomes a game of "wait and see what happens". In this type of experiment, the ghost hunters come to the location, set up monitoring equipment and then wait to see what they record. As mentioned, it can be time-consuming, and more than a bit boring, but the researcher might be surprised at how well it pays off.

Before getting involved in this sort of research, it helps to be able to establish a set pattern for the reported activity. In other words, the witnesses might tell you that certain incidents occur around the same time of the evening. It is also useful research in a fairly active location where phenomena has been widely reported. Every ghost hunter wants to be present when something that cannot be explained actually occurs and can be witnessed and/or captured on film.

There are a couple of different ways to conduct this type of experiment. The first method is the use of monitoring equipment and cameras. While both require equipment, the first method that I want to discuss is more equipment-based than the other. Using this method, the ghost researcher can literally place himself outside of the area of the investigation and monitor it with cameras that will record any activity.

This can be useful for several reasons and there is a system involved for setting things up. Let me give you some ideas to work with:

1. Find a location in the house that is best suited for monitoring. It may be an area where the witnesses report the most activity, or perhaps an area where an earlier sweep of the house picked up some anomalous readings that you could not rule out as artificial disruptions or interference.

2. Using your video camera (or in this case more than one), you will need to be able to run video cables to a monitoring system outside of the room or area. You can pick up any of the equipment that you need for this at a local electronics store and you may want to consider hooking up a recorder that can also record any activity that occurs. Usually, I recommend using more than one monitor for this experiment, perhaps one for each camera.

3. As an alternative, there are a number of companies that offer security and monitoring systems, most of which were designed for retail stores and companies. Some of them even offer night-vision capabilities and infrared filming in total darkness. The systems often come with several cameras and professional monitors that offer multi-screen viewing on one unit. You can also hook up a recorder to these units as well so that you can go back and watch the tape later.

4. Recording the "ghost watch" is essential. As mentioned, you will need to go back and watch the tape later (perhaps even frame by frame) to see what may have occurred that didn't immediately register with the watchers. This is the same as with any investigation that you do, when watching hours of tape may be imperative to your investigation results.

5. After getting your cameras placed, you will need to set up the rest of the equipment. I recommend using Tri-Field Natural EM Meters, which can be used as stationary monitors of energy disruptions in a room. By pointing one of your cameras (and/or sound recording equipment) in the direction of the meters, you

can see any changes that might occur in the location.

You should also consider using a temperature and humidity gauge that can be monitored on camera too. During any investigation, the ghost hunter needs to make note of the temperature of the location and, if possible, the humidity levels. Both readings may have an effect on the outcome of photos, video and monitoring. As any sudden drops in temperature may signal the presence of something anomalous, this might be vital to the experiment's result.

I also recommend the use of infrared motion detectors as well. These units have more than one benefit. By monitoring the infrared spectrum of the location, it's possible that the units might pick up something that is unseen by the human eye. On more than one occasion in the past, ghost hunters have reported inexplicable alarms from these units, even when there was nothing to see. Later, they were surprised to find strange images had appeared in their photos or on video. They also sometimes noted corresponding readings with their detection equipment. In addition, the units can be used to monitor the area for living persons, effectively sealing the area from entry. This is very important when fraud is suspected or when conducting a "ghost watch" experiment where none of the investigators are in the immediate area.

This brings us to the main benefit of this type of experiment. By sealing off the area to everyone and monitoring it from a remote location, the investigator has effectively ruled out a source of activity that could be mistaken for paranormal. As most of us know, the human body emits its share of electromagnetic energy and this could have an effect on the more sensitive meters, including motion detectors and the Natural EM Meter. Also, since no one will be moving through the area, we have a perfect opportunity to monitor an area without human interference. We have then eliminated not only small temperature changes caused by the human body, but we have also eliminated the chance for minute dust particles to be blown into the air. That means that any anomalies that appear on the film from that location have a much better chance of being paranormal.

In many cases though, this type of "ghost watch" may not be practical. Not all ghost hunters are as fully equipped as this method requires and not all home owners are as agreeable as this method would need them to be. Some witnesses are happy to have you at the location, but not in such an invasive manner. As we are always required to honor the wishes of the location owner, we have to adapt our investigations to suit their mood and desires.

For this reason, another method of the "ghost watch" is most often used and I always recommend it to researchers with a more limited budget. In my experience, a "ghost watch" is an essential part of every investigation, or at least those investigations where natural and artificial explanations have been ruled out. If you have managed to get that far with your research, then being present and "waiting for something to happen" should always be the next step. And even if you don't have the funds and equipment for the first type of "ghost watch", you can easily handle the second.

This method can be just as important to the overall investigation and while you will still want to record as much of the event as possible, usually one video camera (or at the most, two) will do the trick. In addition, your still camera will come in handy as well. This method depends more on the alertness and common sense of the ghost hunter than on high-tech equipment. Since it does not involve completely sealing off portions of the house, it is usually more palatable to the home owner too. Here are some details on how best to handle this:

1. As with the previous system, seek out an area of the house / location that you want to monitor. The good news is that this does not have to be a single room, hallway or staircase. Because the monitoring here is done more by man than machine, the investigation team can actually be scattered throughout the location. In this way, you can observe almost the entire house and perhaps even everyone who is in it. By stationing the group in different rooms, the team is in perhaps a better position than any other to decide if the case is genuine or not.

2. If possible, it can't hurt for each of the team members to have their own video camera to record anything (supernatural or otherwise) that might occur in their designated area. If this is not possible though, it is imperative that the team member keeps track of everything that occurs, and everyone who enters, their portion of the house. The investigator's camera will be handy for this as they can actually keep a photographic record of anything that changes in their section and should also consider taking photographs at regular intervals as well. There is no way to know just what might turn up on the film.

3. In spite of the fact that sitting around and waiting for something to happen can be excruciatingly boring over a long period of time, the researcher must stay alert and be prepared for anything. For this reason (if no other), I suggest that team leaders carefully choose group members for investigations. If you know a member is prone to falling asleep, or becomes easily bored, they may not be your best choice to take part in this kind of experiment. For those team members who are videotaping their area, they should keep the camera running at all times. If using night vision technology, I suggest monitoring the camera screen for anything not visible to the human eye. (because this will more rapidly drain the camera battery, consider plugging in to a nearby power source if possible). Those members who are monitoring their areas visually should also remain on high alert and should keep their still camera available at all times. They should also keep a notebook and pen, a tape recorder, and any other ghost hunting equipment close at hand.

This type of experiment might last for hours, or it might last all night. Obviously, there is a very good chance that nothing out of the ordinary will happen but you have to be prepared for it if it does. Team members should be sure to have a good supply of "energy drink" along with them, be it coffee or their favorite soda. It is bound to be a long night and a largely uneventful one.

It is also recommend that one of the team members (a designated leader) check in with the other investigators on a regular basis. This person can provide not only assistance, but perhaps extra film, batteries, refreshments or even encouragement when needed. This can keep the investigators on their toes and wide awake during a lengthy investigation.

I always feel that a designated leader is important to any investigation, and not just so that everyone stays awake. This person can coordinate the investigation, dealing with the owners and planning when everyone should arrive and who should be in charge of what task. This person becomes doubly important during a "ghost watch" because the team has to be properly coordinated for the experiment to have the most benefit.

There are some other things worth thinking about too, no matter what type of "ghost watch" that you decide to experiment with. These are simply some odds and ends and items that are worth keeping in mind:

1. If a "ghost watch" is worth doing once, then it is worth repeating. To get to the point where one of these methods becomes worthwhile, you should be reasonably sure that something is taking place at the location that you cannot explain away as ordinary. Just remember that you should not be disappointed if nothing happens on the first investigation. This is why I always insist on follow-up research at presumably haunted spots. It's likely that your vigilance and persistence will pay off with something in the end. Even if it doesn't though, you will have managed to establish a good pattern for future experiments. Or at the very least, you have done as I have often done --- you have established what not to do the next time.

2. As part of the standard investigation, I always recommend that the team members prepare a diagram of the location on which they can mark questionable areas and spots where they may have picked up anomalies of any sort. These diagrams are especially important during a "ghost watch" and a map of this type can be used to mark designated areas for team members, as well as for any odd happenings.

3. You will need to decide what the investigators should be doing in their designated areas. For the method one "ghost watch", the area is sealed off and there are no investigators present in the monitored location. However, in the second method, the researchers are literally interacting with the location. There

has been much debate as to what works better --- silence or normal behavior. Opinions vary on this and I feel that it really depends on the location itself. In a place where sounds carry in unusual ways (like an old theater), it is probably best that the investigators remain completely silent, or as much so as possible. On other occasions, they might be able to behave normally and quietly in whatever area has been designated to them.

Keep in mind though (especially if you are a leader of an investigation team), your group members will remain much more alert and ready if they are allowed to move about to some extent and behave normally. Working under conditions of silence, and sitting still for hours at a time, can be exhausting. This can lead to errors in observation and leave the investigators stressed out and irritable, which are not the best conditions for a well carried out investigation. A compromise that I might suggest would be to alternate the periods of silence and restricted movement with periods of more normal behavior. You will find that your "ghost watch" can continue much longer this way.

4. Another element to keep in mind during your "ghost watch" is the lighting of the location. While working with the first type of experiment, which depends mainly on the use of cameras and equipment, you may consider working in near or total darkness. This may increase the activity and also increase your chances of recording it. Many ghost hunters prefer to work this way and it can be useful in situations where no one will be walking around or moving around in the monitored areas. There are no concerns of anyone being injured in the dark and your infrared cameras should be able to pick up any anomalous activity, as well as being able to still check the read outs on the equipment that is also under observation.

Obviously, in the other type of "ghost watch", total darkness is not always practical. In the past, I have experimented in both darkness and in low light. While conducting investigations inside of private homes, I have found low lighting to be the preferred method. By keeping the lights low, the investigators will be able to see but their vision (and any photographs that are taken) will not be affected by glare from harsh or too much lighting.

Low lighting is also of assistance in avoiding unwanted attention to your investigation. By having all of the lights turned off and on at a location and having flashlights bouncing around and moving past the windows, the investigation could attract the attention of the neighbors or in the worst case, the police. You can understand how this might look suspicious to someone passing by and this is yet another reason to suggest that the lights remain on but at a discreet level.

Finally, let me make one last mention of a type of "ghost watch" that has not been talked about here so far. This type of "ghost watch" differs from the others because it is designed to be used during a reported poltergeist outbreak. In a situation like this, the investigator has to quickly decide if the reported events are connected to actual ghosts or to one of the people residing in the house. To reach this point, a lot of interviewing and investigation has to be done. If the case is an active one, it is very possible that sounds might occur or physical items might be moved while the investigators are present.

In a situation like this, your "ghost watch" skills become very important. It is essential that team members are stationed throughout the house and that cameras and recording devices are running constantly. In this way, you have the best chance of actually documenting the activity. The most important thing to remember (whether you suspect the case is genuine or a hoax) is to keep the family members under constant observation. By keeping track of the movements of everyone present, you can actually authenticate the events that occur.

However, keeping the family under constant watch does present some problems. Since you do not want to seem like a kidnapper who is holding a group of hostages, you have to be subtle about how you do this. If the homeowners feel that you don't trust them or that you think they are faking the whole thing, then they are likely to become offended and ask you to leave. This is where your repartee with the witnesses comes into play and why everyone ghost hunter has to have some amount of "people skills", or they should not be dealing with the witnesses.

Rather than herd them into a group and stand over them, you should try and engage the family in conversation or explain to them that they should not move around too much with the idea that it might interfere with your testing equipment. Since people don't move around as much when you are talking or interacting with them, I suggest getting them to talk about their interests, school, their jobs, whatever it takes. You might also consider allowing them to "help" with the investigation, keeping notes or making diagrams --- anything that will keep them busy.

If for some reason the "haunting" turns about to be a hoax, this is your best chance of finding that out. There have been many cases that start out with great promise and eventually are revealed to be the antics of an adolescent in the house whose playful pranks went just a bit too far. Although it may be the hardest thing that you have to do, revealing to the parents that you have a video clip of the prankster at work will certainly cure all of the fears that they had of their house being haunted. And if the phenomenon does turn out to be real, then your hours of "ghost watching" have certainly paid off!

CEMETERY RESEARCH: USING YOUR CAMERA

In past editions of some of my ghost hunting manuals, I published some rather scathing comments about the so-called "ghost hunters" who spent their time running about in cemeteries, snapping photographs and calling what they were doing investigations. I received a number of responses to my comments and while some were harsh, many of them were simply looking for more information. If this was not the best way to conduct ghost research in cemeteries, then what was?

A few years ago, I began writing about methods for conducting investigations in cemeteries and other outdoor locations. For the most part, the response for this was positive but many well-established researchers began to criticize me for encouraging people to carry out what they called "useless research". They believe that no legitimate investigations can be carried out in cemeteries but this is mostly because of the way that such investigations were handled in the past.

However, I believe that conducting paranormal research in cemeteries really shouldn't be that much different than conducting an investigation in someone's home or in a building. Every investigation has to be organized and there has to be a point to it, otherwise we can't legitimately call it "research" or even an "investigation". To be able to conduct an actual investigation, we have to have rules and criteria to go by. The ghost hunter should have his own checklist of items to be studied at the site because while wandering around in a cemetery taking pictures is fun, it does not constitute an actual investigation.

The first thing to do when preparing for a cemetery vigil is to choose the site. This should not be done by simply picking a cemetery at random. Despite what some people apparently believe, not every cemetery is haunted. However, there are hundreds of sites where strange stories have been told, dark history has taken place and where people have encountered things that cannot be explained.

Once you do find a place that seems promising, start looking into the history of it so that you can decide if it is a location for legitimate research. You can refer to the *Ghost Hunter's Guidebook* for the best methods of doing this but if your research does lead you to suspect that something ghostly may be taking place at the location, then you should consider organizing an investigation.

Once all of your preliminary research has been finished, there is still much to be done before the actual investigation takes place. Some of that will mean returning to the cemetery for some additional surveying and exploration, although this time it will be specifically in regards to the vigil that your investigation team will be carrying out on the grounds.

You will need to return to the cemetery that you have chosen and you will need to bring your notebook and pen with you. There are a number of things that have to be noted about the graveyard and the surrounding area before you can return at night. Make sure that this step is carried out during the daylight hours so that everything can be seen in detail. You will be coming back after dark for the investigation, so all of this data will need to be compiled now. Here are some steps for you to follow:

1. Draw a map of the location, as close to scale as possible. Be sure to mark any landmarks or noticeable spots on the map so that other team members will be able to easily locate them. This may mean trees, mausoleums, easily identifiable grave markers and monuments and anything else that the team can use to orient themselves between the cemetery and your map.

2. Take note of the location's surroundings. Be sure to notice what might be seen from the location during the investigation. If woods surround the cemetery, check and see if there are houses on the other side of the trees. Even a small amount of light (or sound) from a home or farm could appear to be anomalous in any photos that might be taken or on any recordings that your group might make.

3. Take many photographs of the site in the daytime. That way, any night time photos can be checked for location and compared to areas that might be active.

After leaving the site, there is more preparation work that needs to be done. One of the most important things can be accomplished by speaking with local authorities. It is imperative that if you are planning to conduct an investigation in a public location, you find out what the state and local laws say about trespassing in a cemetery after dark. In most cases, unless the site is otherwise posted, you will be asked to leave the cemetery if bothered by law enforcement officials. If the cemetery is posted, then you could be arrested or fined. Never go into a cemetery that is posted against nighttime trespassing unless you have permission to be there.

4. Try to get permission in writing from the owners of the location to conduct investigations at the site. Few cemeteries are privately owned and most belong to the local community (or the township in rural areas). You can speak to the on-site superintendent about this. You might also contact the local police department as a courtesy and let them know that you will be at the site. This may be very important if you are unable to get written permission. If you can get permission, take the letter with you to the site.

5. After selecting the site and getting your clearances (if applicable), carefully put together a team of people to accompany you to the location. As with any other investigation, you will want to put together people who can take photographs, run the equipment, use the video camera, etc. Be sure not to tell them

what to expect before the vigil. If they witness anything at the site that matches previous reports, this will strengthen your suspicions about the place being haunted.

6. Once your team has been put together, I recommend preparing a variety of equipment that you want to take with you. Your team should be no larger than 7-9 people and no less than 5. Here is a list of some equipment that I believe is worth taking along (in addition to extra batteries and essential items from whatever "ghost hunter's kit" you have devised):

- Flashlights (one for every team member)
- clipboard, paper, pencil & copies of the location maps
- EMF detectors and IR temperature probes
- Cameras (one for every team member)
- At least one video camera, capable of IR filming in total darkness
- PIR (Passive Infrared) motion detectors
- hygrometer (measure humidity in the area)
- Thermometer (check weather conditions for the vigil)

Beyond this basic list, you should add whatever pieces of equipment that you feel would be useful in your particular location or investigation. Just be sure that you have a practice run with any new or unfamiliar equipment prior to the investigation. This is also suggested with new cameras and probes as well. Most likely, you will be working in uncomfortable and dark conditions and it is important that the investigators be familiar with the equipment before arriving at the location.

7. Before you leave for the investigation, consider using the map that you have already made to decide where you would like to first set up the equipment. This might be based on previous reports from the location or insights by the team member who previously visited the site. No matter what, it will give you a place to start from and a "game plan" for the investigation.

Before the investigation actually begins, you may want to go over some ground rules with your team. Here are some suggestions for things to keep in mind while getting the investigation organized:

1. Never take on an investigation like this alone. A good team is required for legitimate research. Not only is safety important in an outdoor or an isolated location, but it is essential to have more than one person to authenticate evidence and incidents that might occur.

2. Never trespass in a location without permission. As mentioned earlier, you should try and get permission from the caretaker of the cemetery, or county officials, before the investigation. If this cannot be done, get in touch with the local police department or sheriff's department about the investigation. This is a good idea to do no matter what, even if for nothing other than courtesy and professionalism.

3. Do not drink or smoke prior to or (especially) during the investigation. The majority of evidence from the night comes in the form of photographs that have been obtained with corresponding evidence. If a team member is smoking, even if the smoke does not appear in any photos, it can destroy the credibility of any evidence that might be obtained.

4. As with any other investigation, arrive at the scene with skepticism and make an effort to find a natural explanation for any phenomena that occurs.

5. During the investigation, be sure to write down and make a note of anything that occurs, no matter how small it seems. I suggest creating a logbook for the investigation. A logbook can be prepared in advance and should contain the following information:

- Date and time of the Investigation
- Name and location of the site
- Investigators / team members present
- Weather conditions (temperature / humidity / barometer readings and even the wind speed... check the local weather service before leaving home)
- Detailed list of the equipment being used

Each of the team members should receive a copy of the log sheet, along with the map of the location. An additional sheet should also be added with times listed along the left side. On the right, blank spaces should be inserted so that any activity that occurs can be noted next to the corresponding time. You need to have a photographic log as well (especially when working with infrared film) so that you can keep track of when and where your photographs were taken.

6. Finally, leave the location exactly as it was when you found it. Be sure that you do not leave any trash behind and also be sure that nothing is done to physically disturb the site, such as knocking over a tombstone. Even accidents can have a grave effect on the opportunity that you might have for future investigations at this site and others.

Once you arrive back at the cemetery that night, you are going to want to get a "feel" for the place and to set up a base of operations. I suggest finding a central location that is easily recognized by all of the team members. Here, you can leave your equipment cases and any non-essential items that do not need to be carried about the cemetery or location. If possible, try to arrive at the site before dark so that all of the team members can get a look at the place. Hopefully, the map that you made will have noted any hazards that might be encountered (like an open grave) but if not, this will give everyone a chance to see things for themselves.

Once this is done, you should start setting up any stationary equipment that you plan to use, like Tri-Field meters and motion detectors. Position the instruments in locations where they will not be moved and have each team member make note of where everything is so that they will not stumble over it later. Make sure the equipment is in a place where it is most likely to encounter phenomena. If nothing occurs after a set period of time (say, one hour), then try moving it to another spot. If the hand-held equipment encounters something in a different place, try moving the stationary equipment to that area as well.

Once the equipment is in place, it is time to get started.

1. It is best to try and split the investigators into separate teams. You may have noticed that when I noted the ideal number of investigators I suggested an odd number of people. I feel that one person should always be in charge of monitoring the stationary equipment. It does not have to be the same person for the entire investigation, but this should always be someone's job. He or she should take notes of anything that occurs and if more than one camera is available, keep a video camera monitoring this equipment.

2. The rest of the researchers should be split up into teams of two and should begin checking out the rest of the location with various other types of equipment. Remember that you are not here to randomly snap photographs! You should be searching for all manner of activity and photographing any anomalies that may occur in order to provide corresponding evidence. It might be best that one member of the team handles the equipment and the other team member holds the flashlight and the investigation log. This person can keep track of anything unusual that occurs and mark the location of the occurrence on the map.

3. Ideally, the vigil will last from 2-4 hours (depending on the amount of activity recorded) and this means that the location will have to be covered almost continuously during this time. Try to refrain from too many breaks and from leaving the equipment unwatched. There is no pattern as to when something paranormal might occur and the investigator has to be constantly aware.

4. If strange activity is found during the course of the night, the investigators should compare notes and try to pinpoint the most active areas of the location. Using the map that you have drawn, it becomes possible to see what areas of the location boast the most anomalies. For the last hour or so of the vigil, it is suggested that all of the equipment and the cameras be focused on this area.

Even though the investigation ends for the night, it is far from over. All of the data that you collected has to be gone over, the tapes watched and the photos developed. In an investigation such as this, you have a unique situation in that you rarely have any eyewitness testimony to collect. For this reason, the material that you have collected becomes even more important and essential to any theories that you might develop about the haunting.

If paranormal occurrences in your cemetery of research do happen, definitely plan to do follow-up investigations. And when you do, you might consider working with different investigators (as well as the same team members) and try to focus your research on the areas of the location that were the most active. You might see an increase in activity, or possibly even a decline. If this occurs, continue the same methods that you used in your initial vigil and see if the phenomena has moved to a different area.

Just remember that an investigation of this sort can quickly deteriorate into a circus if it is not handled properly. It is extremely important that the goals of the group remain focused and that the vigil is organized and well thought out. This is the only way that an outdoor, or cemetery, investigation can be considered successful and the only way that it can be considered to be legitimate ghost research.

5. GHOSTS ON FILM: ANALYZING THE EVIDENCE

The photography of spontaneous ghosts is a chancy and unreliable business… Photographs of ghosts may be the most valuable independent evidence yet obtainable, but the malicious production of so-called 'ghost photographs' is notoriously easy and, in some cases, the results are extremely convincing to anyone other than a person experienced in photography and fraud.

Peter Underwood

As has already been mentioned in this book, expect to use a lot of film when attempting spirit photography because most of the photos that you take will contain nothing out of the ordinary at all. As an extension of that, plan to also look at a lot of photos that have nothing paranormal in them as well. There are thousands of photos that have been taken, while attempting to photograph ghosts, that are nothing more than bad pictures, contain images that can be mistaken for something paranormal or are examples of outright fraud.

The first thing that you need whenever you are attempting to analyze your own photos, or someone else's, is a copy of the photograph and the negative. You have to be sure that the image that appears in the photo is on the negative as well, whether it is a developing flaw or someone who has gotten "creative" with a photo print and wants you to believe that they have photographed a ghost. Many people will like you to analyze their photos via email, whether they are scanned prints or digital images, but this is hard to do. Photos rarely look the same on a computer monitor as they do when looking at them firsthand but you might be able to preview a photo that they want to send to you. That way, if it's something that is easily explainable, no one has to waste any time with further examination. If the photo is a digital image only, the only way to authenticate it is to study the EXIF information the image contains, which normally has to be done with the camera itself. However, there are other factors that are extremely important.

The conditions under which the photo was taken is extremely important.

Researchers should always use a photographic log when taking pictures during an investigation but the average person with an unusual photo will have to try and remember what was taking place when the snapshot was taken. Some of the most important factors are weather conditions, temperature, humidity, what was going on at the time, where the photo was taken and more. It should also be noted what type of camera was being used, the film speed, whether or not the flash was on and anything else that can be remembered. In addition, why was the photo taken in the first place? Was it during an investigation, as an attempt to photograph a ghost, and did the photographer know the location had a reputation for being haunted? Or was the photo taken at a home or location where no activity has ever been reported?

Here are some things to look for when you are trying to determine whether or not the photos that you analyze have natural --- or accidental --- explanations:

1. OUT OF FOCUS PHOTOS: Many "spirit photographs" that people believe are ghosts are often nothing more than blurred or out of focus pictures. There are many reasons why this can be caused. Many pictures are blurred when the lens is set at the wrong distance, when the subject is too close to a fixed lens camera or when the subject moves too quickly while the shutter is open. Moving subjects require fast shutter speeds and the faster the subject is moving, the higher the shutter speed required. Blurred can also happen when the photographer accidentally moves the camera as well. This can be stopped by using a tripod or just by being much more careful about hand movement while using the camera.

2. DIRTY CAMERA LENS: A dirty camera lens can cause all manner of problems, from blurred images to "mysterious" spots that appear in your pictures. The best way to avoid this is to always make sure that the camera lens is clean. Never touch the lens with a finger though. Always use a cloth or soft brush that is designed to be used on the sensitive glass. Spots that appear in your photos may be caused by dust particles or something else that ended up on the lens.

3. LIGHT DAMAGED FILM: Obviously, photographic film is very sensitive to light, since this is essentially how photography works in the first place. Any unwanted light that connects to the film can cause damage to the photos or can ruin them altogether. A large amount of light that strikes the film can cause it to turn black and no photos will be available for development at all. Even if it does not destroy the film completely, it's possible that reddish streaks will appear on the photos. This can often occur when loading or unloading film in bright light, which is why it is recommended that cameras be loaded in subdued lighting conditions.

4. SCRATCHED FILM: There are a couple of different ways that scratches can appear on photos and often these scratches are mistaken for something unusual. They often show up as a sharp line, or lines, that cross the image on the film. The scratches can be caused by dirt inside of the camera back, rough rewinding of the film or during the development process. The best way to see if the images in the film are caused by scratches is to see if the marks are on the negative and the print, or just the print alone. If the scratches are just on the print, then it means that it occurred during the processing. Reprinting can correct this problem if the image continues to be a concern. If the scratches appear on the negative, a check of the camera might reveal a rough spot in the film path.

5. OBJECTS IN THE LENS: Earlier in the book, in the section of hints and tips for successful picture taking, I warned against anything that might protrude in front of the camera lens during photography. As so many alleged "ghost photos" are nothing more than fingers, hair and clothing that has ended up in front of the camera, I felt that it was worth mentioning it again. An object that appears in front of the lens can be dark or black in color and usually has a hazy outline to it. These same objects, when illuminated by the camera flash, appear to be brightly lit and white in color. This is why so many camera straps have been mistaken for "vortexes" (whatever they are!) because they seem to be in motion and "glowing white". Camera straps seem to be the most commonly mistaken objects to appear in "ghost photos" so be sure to leave your camera strap around your neck where it belongs.

6. FLASH REFLECTIONS & REFRACTIONS: Although this has already been discussed in the earlier section about "orbs" and false images that are mistaken for something paranormal, it should be mentioned again in the analysis section. These reflections and lens refractions are often mistaken for ghosts and end up on film when the camera flash reflects from polished surfaces like mirrors, metals, polished wood and even tombstones. In many cases, even artificial light can cause these images to appear, as can the sun when it reflects off something and then bounces off the lens. This is definitely something to watch for (along with dust and pollen) when someone sends you a photo of their "orbs" to look at.

7. DOUBLE EXPOSURES: Double-exposed photographs occur when the film in the camera is not fully advanced all of the way or not advanced at all. Sometimes the last picture on the roll will overlap the second to the last picture and this causes images from both photos to blend together into one. Usually, this is blatantly obvious but in some cases, a subject from one photo will "mysteriously" appear in the other, looking like a transparent person --- or a ghost. Later in this chapter, we will discuss how this can be done on purpose when someone is attempting a "ghostly hoax".

8. DEVELOPING PROBLEMS: Unfortunately, there are many things that can go wrong during the developing process that can cause otherwise ordinary photographs to appear paranormal. Thankfully though, modern developing processes are much more sophisticated than they used to be. In spite of this, things can still go wrong. Uneven densities in the print can be caused by the uneven development of the negative. Stains and marks that appear on the print can be caused by inefficient rinsing and even weird colors in your photos can be caused by bad paper or improper developing. In most cases, developing problems are easy to spot and are rarely ever mistaken for anything paranormal. Mistakes do happen though - so always be careful!

As the reader can see from this section, as well as from other sections of the book, many things can go wrong when attempting spirit photography and it's hard to stress enough just how rare authentic paranormal photographs actually are. As mentioned, it often takes hundreds of attempts before the photographer obtains even a single image that cannot be easily explained away by one of the just mentioned problems --- as well as rain, natural fogs, cigarette smoke and a variety of other issues.

Just remember that every photo that is alleged to be something paranormal should be intensely analyzed by the researcher before he is willing to state that it contains a ghost or anything unexplained at all. There are hundreds of terrible photos out there that claim to be authentic. Most of them are not, which is why it is so important to be careful with any pictures that you have. If you are analyzing photos be sure that you have a good working knowledge of cameras, films and lens effects. You should know your camera, your shutter speeds and what can happen with lens refractions, light reflections and arcs. By doing this, you have protected yourself from the arguments of the debunkers and perhaps have spared yourself some embarrassment by finding flaws in some of your own photos. Once you understand the natural effects that can occur, you will be confident about the photos you are taking.

"CREATING GHOSTS": FRAUDULENT GHOST PHOTOS

Most photographs that are mistakenly believed to be ghosts are the result of accidents, mistakes and a lack of knowledge. It's rare that someone actually attempts to hoax a ghost photo and pawn it off on an investigator as the real thing. But believe me, as I can tell you from experience, it does happen. Whoever said that "pictures never lie" was obviously not someone with photographic experience. Almost everyone knows that a photo can be easily faked. One way, which involves techniques using the camera, the darkroom and other means, is by combining images. There are also camera tricks, darkroom deceptions, retouching and computer enhancements as well.

In many cases, it's very hard to tell when a photo has been doctored --- and a ghost "created" ---- but it's certainly not impossible. There are ways to detect trickery in photographs (both paranormal photographs and otherwise) and the rest of this chapter will take a look at some of them.

1. COMBINING IMAGES: Among the oldest photographic tricks in existence is combining two or more images to make a composite. One of the simplest ways of doing this does not require either camera or darkroom fakery and dates back to the days of studio photography in the late 1800's. Many portraits of the day were created by posing the subject in front of a scenic or pictorial backdrop that created the illusion that the people were part of the scene. There were wilderness scenes, lakeside scenes, drawing rooms, libraries filled with books and even military and camp scenes. In their modern form, these composite scenes (as they are called) may be produced by front or rear projection.

2. COLLAGES: Another type of historic photo trickery is the collage, which was also carried out without the use of a camera or darkroom effort. In times past, the hoaxer merely cut images out of one photo and pasted them onto another. Then, he would touch up the images to smooth out the lines and then would re-photograph it to produce a negative and make prints from it. Today, this process is much easier than it was years ago. All that is required now is a couple of digital images from which one image can be cut out and "pasted" into another one. To the naked eye, this deception can often go unnoticed, which is why the digital date files produced by newer cameras can be so important. However, if the combined images were created using scanned prints and then combined, things can be much trickier. It's suggested that the researcher gain a good working knowledge of digital photo programs that will allow him to take images apart, layer by layer, and reveal whatever trickery may be involved.

3. MULTIPLE / DOUBLE EXPOSURES: Although discussed earlier in the chapter as being accidentally produced, double exposure photos can be made for deceptive reasons as well. In fact, most "ghost photos" that have been created as a hoax have been done using this method. In the past, double exposures were easily created by simply not winding the film onto the next exposure. This could be done inadvertently or on purpose but these days, most modern cameras have features to prevent repeat exposures. However, even these cameras can be fooled into not advancing onto the next frame. Digital cameras can also be used in this manner but most multiple exposures with digital technology are created after the fact. Using a digital photo program (as mentioned in the last section) makes it possible to combine several images into one --- creating another fraudulent ghost photo.

And even though it has been said many times over the years that you cannot double expose a Polaroid photo, this is unfortunately not the case. The mechanisms of Polaroid cameras can be circumvented too. By taking photos with the film door open (and placing black tape across the front of the film pack to prevent light leakage), the exposed picture can be prevented from being fed out and developed. Then, a second exposure can be made the same way. With older Polaroid cameras, a double exposure was even simpler to accomplish. There was a lever on the right side of the camera that cocked the shutter. After the shutter release button was pressed, all that had to be done to create a double exposed photo was to cock the shutter again and take another picture.

4. LONG EXPOSURE PICTURES: This is another method of creating "ghost photos" that has been around for a very long time. In the early chapters of the book, during the discussion on the history of spirit photography, it was mentioned that some fraudulent photos were created by opening the shutter of the camera and allowing an assistant to enter the frame for a few moments and then stepping out. With a long shutter exposure, this created a semi-transparent figure that seemed to materialize within the solid setting of the studio. This is easily done today with just about any SLR camera. Using a tripod, the camera is set up and the shutter opened. A person walks through the frame for a moment, creating an image that shows up on the finished print --- creating a ghost.

DETECTING TRICKERY

It may not always be possible to detect trickery in a photograph. It could be a straightforward, untouched photo in which a scene was staged or faked in some way. As mentioned already, it's nearly impossible to detect computer trickery in many cases. Regardless, there are procedures and techniques for detecting many kinds of photo hoaxes that involve checking the source of the photo, the circumstances behind it, checking the negatives and more. In some cases, the same techniques that we use in detecting accidental photos also apply because we can never be too careful when it comes to searching for authentic examples of the paranormal.

1. INVESTIGATING THE SOURCE: With any photo that you have questions about, always consider the source of it. If the photo "seems too good to be true", it likely is, especially when it's a case when the person with the photo cannot, or will not, tell you where the photo came from. It's also not uncommon for photos to make the rounds on the Internet that seem to have no source of where they came from. One such example was one that was being sent out with the claim that if you did not pass it on to someone else, you would have terrible luck. The photo was alleged to have come from an Asian country and showed a young man with a very evil-looking female ghost hovering behind him. In some versions of the accompanying story, the young man died shortly after the photo was taken. This is a great example of not only a fake photo, but an Internet "urban legend" as well. The fact that the photo had no clear source pointed to its dubious origins.

In other cases, even possibly authentic photos have to be questioned because of their lack of a reliable source. This can be heartbreaking, especially when the photo just might be real. I ran across a great example of this when some friends sent me a series of photos, one of which seemed to show the ghostly image of a woman inside of a burning house. As far as I could tell, the photo showed no signs of manipulation but when I tried to track down the story behind it, I was given a number of different sources and explanations. One person explained that the photo had come from a minister in Tennessee. Another claimed that it was taken by a minister in Indiana. One said the house belonged to the minister's mother, his grandmother, etc. Without an authentic source, there was no way to accept the photo as genuine, which is a shame.

I have also discovered that by checking with other researchers, you can eliminate some of the questions that you might have regarding a photo's source. On a couple of occasions, friends and fellow ghost hunters have been able to warn me about not only the photos that I asked them about (which had been submitted to them too) but about the source of the photos as well. In both situations, the researchers had already encountered the owners of the photos in the past and it turned out that they had been known for offering fake pictures as genuine.

2. INVESTIGATING THE CIRCUMSTANCES: Although it was mentioned earlier, a good analyst needs to learn everything that he can about the how and why a photo was taken. If the owner of the photo states that he snapped a photo of a ghost in a cemetery on a sunny day but you check the weather report and see that it was raining, you should be cautious about what else he may be mistaken about. Was the photo taken by accident or was the photographer purposely trying to snap a photo of a ghost? Study the photo itself and look for problems when the "ghost" is perfectly framed. Once again, if it looks "too good to be true" --- it probably is.

3. INVESTIGATING THE NEGATIVES: As mentioned previously, a researcher should always obtain the negatives to any photo in question. This is a way to look for not only accidental problems that create a "ghost" but also a good way to detect trickery. The negatives may show actual retouching or yield evidence (like the edge of a photo within the negative's image area) that another photo was copied. If the photo owner refuses to give up the negative, or no negative exists, there is really no way to accept that the image may be genuine.

In a best case scenario, an investigator should insist on examining the negatives from the entire roll of film on which the photo in question was imprinted. These negatives will likely be cut into filmstrips that are cut from the roll and in this case, it's important to make certain that every numbered frame is accounted for and that the cut ends of the strip actually match, since it would be possible to substitute one strip of film from another roll. By studying the sequence of the photos, it might be possible to see if trickery has taken place. It's possible that the negatives might reveal practice shots that were done in advance of the hoax or you might also find that the sequence of the photos does not match the photo owner's story.

GHOSTS ON FILM .... OR NOT

So, when someone brings you a photo to analyze, is it the best to automatically suspect that they are trying to perpetrate a hoax? Not likely - in most cases, the people who take these mysterious photos truly believe they have captured something otherworldly on film. The thing to remember though is that there are many more natural images that occur than supernatural ones.

Chances are you are going to offend someone who has submitted what they believe to be a genuine image but clearly is not one. Many people think they have a "real photo of a ghost" and are unwilling to consider the alternative. A lot of these folks become very offended when you suggest the possible natural causes for the images on their photos. I have found that it's often best to simply be interested but noncommittal when someone brings one of their ghostly photos to you. You should only offer an opinion when someone specifically asks for it and even then, preface your comments by explaining that there are no "experts" when it comes to spirit photography and that you are only basing your comments on your past experience with photographs and possible paranormal images. In that way, you can show the person that you are interested in what they have but can't commit to it without further examination.

But even that further examination can be a problem. Many people will never remember what they were doing or what was going on when the photo was taken. Others will swear that no one there was smoking, regardless of the ashtray that is clearly sitting on the table in the picture. They will tell you that their camera has no strap, that it was not cold outside or that it was not raining and they definitely did not use their camera flash. All that you can do is use your best judgment with the photo and offer the best suggestions that you can. They will either accept them - or they won't. Either way, you have been able to put your skills into use and should you run across a genuine paranormal photo, then all of the work and effort that you have put forth will be well served.

6. GHOSTS ON FILM: ONE LAST LOOK

The majority of photographs purporting
to depict spontaneous ghosts are not genuine
but a few are neither proved to be fakes nor
can be attributed to some fault in the camera,
the film or the taking of the photograph.
There are in existence photographs apparently
depicting ghosts that are very difficult to
explain in rational terms.
Peter Underwood

Nothing can be more convincing than
authentic, genuine evidence of that world "next door" than photographs
--- provided they are taken under conditions excluding any and all possibility of conscious fraud, unconscious delusion and any explanation of
them other than that they are indeed the real pictures of people who
have gone from this world into the next.
Hans Holzer

Over the last two decades or so, since I have been pursuing my interest in ghosts and the supernatural, I have run across quite a decent number of what I feel are authentic ghost photos. Many of them appeared in the earlier chapters of this book as examples of not only history's best spirit photographs but also in the sections that illustrated different types of anomalies that can turn up in pictures. With these last few pages, I wanted to present another small collection of photos that I have come to believe are genuine.

I wish that I could display all of the great photos that I have collected over the years, from my own research and from photos that people have given to me, but unfortunately, many of them don't translate well into print or into black and white. However, I have included another half dozen or so pictures that I think will certainly interest you.

This first photograph was taken and submitted to me by Chris Kirby, one of the owners of the famous Bell Witch Cave near Adams, Tennessee. As most readers are aware, the cave and the former farm of John Bell has a very long history of hauntings and strange activity. I have written about this case very extensively over the years (including in my book *Season of the Witch*) and have visited and investigated the farm many times.

This photo was taken near a sinkhole on the Kirby's farm that leads down into the depths of the haunted cave. The cave itself, while formed by water from limestone, is what is referred to by geologists as a "dry cave". This means that the cave, except for during flood seasons, remains relatively dry and does not have an extensive collection of the common cave features that are formed by water like stalactites and stalagmites. I mention this to dispel the idea that this might be some kind of mist of wet fog that is emerging from the cave via the sinkhole. Many debunkers, who are ignorant and uninformed of the area and the cave's geology, have tried to dismiss this as mere fog.

This image could not be seen by the naked eye when the photo was taken. Some have suggested that they can see the image of a face inside of the ecto-plasmic-like cloud but regardless the source of the "mist" remains unexplained. In 1997, the photo was submitted to the Kodak Laboratories and they had no explanation for it and could find nothing wrong with the film, negative or print that would debunk this image.

The next photograph was submitted to me by Helen Sievers, a long-time paranormal investigator and a representative for the American Ghost Society in New York state. The baby in the photo is Helen's daughter and it was taken nearly 25 years ago when she was only 9 months old.

The glare that you see in the lower part of the photo (left side) is obviously

the glare from the flash of the camera as it reflects in the sliding glass door, however, I do not believe that the image that appears on the left side of the photo was caused by the flash. It does not appear to be a refraction on the camera lens, as many "orb" photos actually are. The anomalous area appears to have multi-dimensional qualities and has a shape unlike that of camera flare. It also does not appear to be a reflection on the glass as the body of the baby stands between the glass flare and the anomalous image.

There does not appear to be an explanation for this picture.

This next series of images was actually submitted to me in video form by Chris Puckett, the owner of a salvage yard in Oklahoma City, Oklahoma. Many readers may recognize this strange and controversial image and while I cannot say for sure that it is genuine, I will say that when investigating the source of the images, I found no reason why the owner would lie about them or attempt to perpetrate a hoax of some sort. The video, which was taken from surveillance cameras at the salvage yard, received national attention back in 2002 but it was not because the owner sought out the press. Actually, no one would have ever learned about it if not for the fact that emergency workers and tow truck drivers, who regularly came to the salvage yard, saw the video and leaked the story to the press.

Video Courtesy Puckett Auto

The bizarre video of what seemed to be a floating apparition of some sort first came to the public's attention when Oklahoma City's NBC news affiliate broadcast the footage on July 24. The report claimed that employees at the auto salvage yard believed they had been visited by the ghost of a woman who had been involved in a fatal car accident.

Video Courtesy Puckett Auto

The image was first seen by an overnight dispatcher named Cathy Henley, who watched it on her monitors as it circled around through the cars. A security guard was sent out to investigate but there was nothing to see when he arrived. As it turned out though, the image was captured on the video recorder that was attached to the security camera. Those who saw the image came to believe that the figure was a ghost.

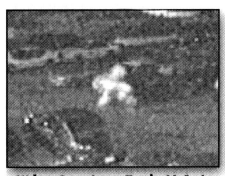

Video Courtesy Puckett Auto

According to sources, the yard had three cars that had been involved in fatal accidents that night. One paranormal investigator speculated that the image might be one of the fatalities searching for its car. Many came to believe that the ghost might be that of a 33-year-old woman named Tracy Martin, who had died on June 30 from injuries that she sustained in her accident. Tracy's wrecked truck had been removed from the same area where the figure was seen just three hours prior to the sighting on July 17.

After seeing the video footage, Tracy's father, brother and husband were said to be convinced that the image was Tracy in her favorite overalls, returning to the scene to let them know she was okay. Others have speculated that her ghost may have been attached to the vehicle because of the sudden loss of her life and it had remained in the salvage yard after the insurance company towed the vehicle away. Whatever the reason though, video surveillance has never captured anything else out of the ordinary in the salvage yard. This was apparently a one-time occurrence.

This next set of images (above) was submitted to me by Angie Ferrer, a ghost researcher in Texas, who captured these four frames with her Sony Night Vision Camera. She and other members of her team had been investigating a house in Killeen Texas off and on for a few months and had previously obtained some interesting video and a collection of anomalies that led them to suspect that genuine activity was occurring in the home. The video clips were captured when the group began experiments to see if they could film strange images at the same time with different video cameras from different angles.

If you take a look at the video clips, which were shot using a Sony Night Vision Camera, you will see the movement of the anomalous object as it literally crosses the camera field in subsequent frames of film. No explanation has been discovered as to what this object might be.

The following photo was sent to me by a website visitor who wanted to share the image and get some thoughts and opinions on it. He wrote: "Inside, you will find a copy of a photo that is very interesting. This cabin is the cabin my

father was born in. It is located in Southern Missouri adjacent to the Johnson Shuttins at Black Missouri.

"My grandmother, now 88, bought back the old farm in the early 1980s. She and her sister, Pauline, spent many weekends restoring the old cabin. As they left the farm one weekend in 1984, Pauline snapped this photo with an instamatic camera. She gave the photo to my grandmother who didn't bother looking at it until she was back at her home in Chester, Illinois.

" I had always heard about the photo and that grandma and Pauline believed it shows their mother in the window. But I didn't actually see it until April 8, 2004, during a visit to grandma's. It was so impressive I just had to send you a copy.

"The window side of the cabin is facing north. At the time of the photo there was no electricity in the house nor external lights. There were also no win-

143

dow shades on the window. A queen size bed is directly along the wall on the inside of the window. I've camped there before but never heard nor saw anything strange."

This next photo was submitted to me by my friends and paranormal researchers, John and Kelly Weaver, who are representatives for the American Ghost Society in Pennsylvania. The photo was taken at Alfred's Victorian Restaurant in Middletown, Pennsylvania.

The town of Middletown was founded in 1755 and Union Street, where Alfred's is located, was the most fashionable boulevard west of Philadelphia during the Victorian era. Built in 1888 by Charles Raymond, the house was full of luxuries. Mr. Raymond's extravagance was his own undoing and in 1896 the house went to the Middletown National bank to benefit his creditors. In 1898, Redsecker Young purchased the dwelling for $6,600. Four years later, the prominent Simon Cameron Young bought it, eventually bequeathing it unto his daughters Emma and Eliza. In 1949, Herman and Sara Baum began their twenty-year residence in the home. Although it had been allowed to deteriorate, the original craftsmanship which made the house so beautiful was still intact. The place was later renovated and turned into a restaurant --- with a long history of haunting activity.

The resident ghost here has been nicknamed "Emma". According to the stories, Emma committed suicide many years ago after being jilted by a lover. Another version states that her fiancé died in the war and she was so despondent that she took her own life. She is said to have thrown herself into the furnace. The basement is a creepy place and no one likes to go down there to use the employee restroom or visit the wine cellar. One server told Kelly that they were mysteriously locked in the wine cellar by an unseen force. It wasn't until another employee came down and heard her screaming for help that she managed to get out of the room.

John Weaver wrote about this photo: "Despite all the activity here, clearly suggestive of an 'Intelligent' haunting, surprisingly little hard evidence has been obtained. I've observed some wild EM field fluctuations, but never got anything good on video. Only a few bright, yet suspect "orbs" have been captured by film and digital cameras but there is one photo that I feel makes a strong case for being "Emma". It is a 35mm image taken by Pamm Yascavage (the owner's daughter) late one evening while standing on the landing of the main staircase. The wait staff is assembled below and a translucent blue streak is seen following the path of the stairs."

This photo has appeared in a number of books, in newspapers and on television shows over the years and despite a couple of different claims of ownership, the photo was taken by a woman named Judi Huff-Felz in August 1991. While involved in a paranormal investigation of i n f a m o u s Bachelor's Grove Cemetery near Chicago, she snapped a photo that has become known as one of the most stunning ghost photos in existence.

Along with the paranormal group she was with at the time, Judi came to the burial ground during the daytime and, with the others in the group, took part in covering the area with scientific equipment, cameras, tape recorders and video cameras. All of the investigators were given maps of the cemetery and instructed to walk through and note any changes in electro-magnetic readings or atmosphere fluctuations. After the maps were compared, it was obvious that several investigators found odd changes in a

145

number of distinct areas. A number of photos were taken in those areas, using both standard and infrared film. Nothing was seen at the time the photographs were taken, but once they were developed, the investigators learned that something had apparently been there.

In this photo, there appeared the semi-transparent form of a woman, who was seated on the remains of a tombstone. Was this one of the ghosts of Bachelor's Grove? Skeptics immediately said "no", claiming that it was nothing more than a double exposure or an outright hoax.

Curious, I later received a copy of the photograph and had it examined by several independent photographers. Most of them would have liked to come up with a reason why the photograph could not be real, but unfortunately they couldn't. They ruled out the idea of a double exposure and also the theory that the person in the photo was a live woman who was placed in the photo and made to appear like she was a ghost. One skeptic also claimed that the woman in the photo was casting a shadow, but according to the photographers who analyzed the image, the "shadow" is actually nothing more than the natural shading of the landscape. Besides that, one of them asked, if she is casting a shadow in that direction, then why isn't anything else in the frame doing the same?

Genuine or not (and I think it is), this photograph is just one of the hundreds of photos taken here that allegedly show supernatural activity. While many of them can be ruled out as nothing more than atmospheric conditions, reflections and poor photography, there are others that cannot. This would definitely be one of them!

This last photo (next page) is one of my favorites and it was submitted to me by American Ghost Society representative Joe Whitfield on behalf of the woman (far right in photo) who wished to remain anonymous. The faces in the photo have been blocked out to conceal the identities of those pictured here.

The photo was taken in 1939 by a man who was known for being kind to hoboes and those down on their luck. He often provided work and meals for them when possible. Family members who still have the photo believe that the "guest" who appears at the far left may be one of these hoboes who passed on before he could return to the place where he always knew kindness.

When I first saw the photo, I was convinced that it was nothing more than a slow shutter and a person who moved while the photo was being taken but after continued examination, I am not so sure. Note the position of the camera and how the subjects are framed. Obviously, the photographer was attempting to take a picture of the three people in the center of the print. This would have made the photograph very unbalanced if someone actually had been sitting on the chair to the left. The woman who submitted the photo to Joe recalls that only three of them were present that day -- making this a very odd and very intriguing photograph.

BIBLIOGRAPHY & RECOMMENDED READING

Auerbach, Loyd - ESP, Hauntings and Poltergeists (1986)
Baker, Robert A. & Joe Nickell - Missing Pieces (1992)
Brugioni, Dino - Photo Fakery (1999)
Coates, James - Photographing the Invisible (1921)
Cohen, Daniel - Encyclopedia of Ghosts (1984)
Cornell, Tony - Investigating the Paranormal (2002)
Doyle, Sir Arthur Conan - The Coming of the Fairies (1922)
Doyle, Sir Arthur Conan - The Edge of the Unknown (1930)
Gettings, Fred - Ghosts in Photographs (1978)
Grimm, Tom & Michelle Grimm - Basic Book of Photography (2000)
Guiley, Rosemary Ellen - Encyclopedia of Ghosts and Spirits (1992 / 2000)
Haining, Peter - Ghosts: The Illustrated History (1987)
Holzer, Hans - America's Restless Ghosts (1993 edition)
 Hope, Valerie & Maurice Townsend - Paranormal Investigator's Handbook (1999)
Kaczmarek, Dale - Field Guide to Spirit Photography (2002)
Nickell, Joe - Camera Clues
Nickell, Joe - Entities (1995)
Ogden, Tom - Complete Idiot's Guide to Ghosts & Hauntings (2000)
Owen, George and Victor Sims - Science and the Spook (1971)
Permutt, Cyril - Photographing the Spirit World (1983)
Price, Harry - Confessions of a Ghost Hunter (1936)
Rogo, D. Scott - An Experience of Phantoms (1974)
Rogo, D. Scott - The Haunted House Handbook (1978)
Rogo, D. Scott - The Haunted Universe (1977)
Roll, William Ph.D. & Valerie Story - Unleashed (2004)
Rule, Leslie - Ghosts Among Us (2004)
Spencer, John and Tony Wells - Ghost Watching (1994)
Taylor, Troy - Confessions of a Ghost Hunter (2002)
Taylor, Troy - Field Guide to Haunted Graveyards (2003)
Taylor, Troy - The Ghost Hunter's Guidebook (1999 / 2001)
Underwood, Peter - Ghosts and How to See Them (1993)
Underwood, Peter - Nights in Haunted Houses (1994)
White, Laurie - Infrared Photography Handbook (1995)
Wilson, Ian - In Search of Ghosts (1995)

Personal Interviews & Correspondence

Special Thanks to:
Kim Young - Proofreading & Editing Services
Vince Wilson
Chris Moseley
Russell White
Ursula Bielski
and Haven Starrett

Note: Although Whitechapel Productions Press, Troy Taylor and all affiliated with this book have carefully researched all sources to insure the accuracy and the completeness of all information contained here, we assume no responsibility for errors, inaccuracies or omissions.

ABOUT WHITECHAPEL PRODUCTIONS PRESS

Whitechapel Productions Press is a small publisher, specializing in books about ghosts and hauntings. Since 1993, the company has been one of America's leading publishers of supernatural books.

Visit Whitechapel Productions Press online and browse through our selection of ghostly titles, plus get information on ghosts and hauntings, haunted history, spirit photographs, information on ghost hunting and much more.

Visit the Internet web page at:

www.historyandhauntings.com

Whitechapel Press is also connected to the acclaimed History & Hauntings Ghost Tours of Alton, Illinois, which were created by Troy Taylor. The tours are an interactive experience that allow readers to visit the historically haunted locations of the city and can be booked between April and July and in October. We are also home to Troy Taylor & Ursula Bielski's Bump in the Night Ghost Tour Co., which offers Haunted Overnight Excursions to ghostly places around the Midwest and throughout the country.

Information on our books and tours are available on the website.

ABOUT THE AUTHOR - TROY TAYLOR

Troy Taylor is the author of 37 books about history, hauntings and the unexplained in America, including HAUNTED ILLINOIS, HAUNTED CHICAGO, WEIRD ILLINOIS and many others. He is also the editor of GHOSTS OF THE PRAIRIE Magazine, about the history, hauntings & unsolved mysteries of America. A number of his articles have been published here and in other publications.

Along with writing about the unusual, Taylor is also a public speaker on the subject and has spoken to literally hundreds of private and public groups on a variety of paranormal subjects. He has appeared in newspaper and magazine articles about ghosts and hauntings. He has also been fortunate enough to be interviewed hundreds of times for radio and television broadcasts about the supernatural. He has also appeared in a number of documentary films, several television series and in one feature film.

Born and raised in Illinois, Taylor has long had an affinity for "things that go bump in the night" and published his first book in 1995. For seven years, he was also the host of the popular, and award-winning, "Haunted Decatur" ghost tours of the city for which he sometimes still appears as a guest host. He also hosted tours in St. Louis and St. Charles, Missouri, as well as in Alton and Chicago, Illinois. Along with fellow author and writing partner Ursula Bielski, he is also co-owner of the Bump in the Night Tour Co., which hosts overnight excursions to haunted places throughout the Midwest.

He currently resides in Central Illinois in a decidedly non-haunted house.

Printed in the United States
36954LVS00006B/7-159

9 781892 523396